OPERATION
MANNA/CHOWHOUND

29th April 1945

Swarms of swallows bringing food
Visions of victory,
Thoughts of freedom
For the starving,
For the powerless,
For the discouraged ones.
They all laugh and cry . . .

They waved from bridges
From canals
From squares and viaducts
They climbed on roof tops
Once bended down they straightened their
backs again
And shook hands

And cheered at every place
For this was a miracle
Salvation from above
Manna-rain
Bringing relief, true blessing
Mighty moment
We waited for months to see it

Elisabeth van Maasdijk
(from 'To the ones who fell', The Hague 1945)

OPERATION MANNA/CHOWHOUND

THE ALLIED FOOD DROPPINGS APRIL/MAY 1945

HANS ONDERWATER

First published in 1985 by
Roman Luchvaart, Unieboek bv, Weesp, The Netherlands.

This edition published in 1991 by
Midland Counties Publications (Aerophile) Limited
24 The Hollow, Earl Shilton, Leicester, LE9 7NA, England
in co-operation with The Manna Association.

Printed in England by Printhaus Litho, Wellingborough, Northants.

Distributed in the USA by
Specialty Press, Publishers & Wholesalers, Inc.
123 North Second Street, Stillwater, MN 55082, USA.

ISBN 0 904597 79 2
© The Manna Association

Contents

Foreword

As an Air Commodore responsible for the Operations and Plans of the Second Tactical Air Force RAF from April 1, 1943 until VE-day I experienced many mixed feelings when dealing with the variety of widely conceived plans which had to be turned into successful operations. In detail, every operation had its lethal aspect with the horrible underlying question which had to be considered in each case – 'Can we ensure that this operation will kill more of the enemy than of our own people?' The one exception where this question did not apply, as far as I can remember, was Operation Manna; the Allied dropping emergency rations from the air with the positive expectation that about 3,500,000 of our friends in the Netherlands could be saved from almost certain death by starvation.

Apart from the actual arrival of the 'Manna' from heaven, dropped by the RAF and USAAF, the air-drops meant that those of our friends who were so forlorn and starving in enemy occupied territory were able to see the Allied aircraft flying low and unhindered over their land, thus conveying to them the life-giving promise that freedom was very close.

I have been thankful that I was able to play a humble part in organizing the drop-zones throughout the occupied part of the Netherlands, to provide a wide range of dropping places by overcoming with facts and figures the objections the Germans tried to make against their use. To me 'Operation Manna' was as worthwhile and as historically important as the D-Day invasion, especially since we had so very little time to lay on the operation.

With respect, great credit is due to His Royal Highness Prince Bernhard of the Netherlands, who was the 'linch-pin' of the very complex organization involved in getting the foodstuffs delivered from the airfields to the actual distribution points in the occupied territory. Many Netherlanders should be grateful to him for his enthusiasm and sense of urgency which inspired us all to save their parents and grandparents who survived those dreadful months in 1945.

'Roseland', Seaford
Andrew James Wray Geddes
Air Commodore CBE, DSO,
Legion of Merit (USA), RAF (retd)

Preface

The weather was good on 24th April 1945. The airspace remained surprisingly empty, much emptier than had been the case in the months preceeding. The news was still good. One third of Berlin is in Russian hands. The Americans are in Ulm. Appingedam is liberated and there is heavy fighting at Delfzijl.

While the British BBC broadcaster reads this news aloud, a few high-flying airplanes trace a path above Western Holland, their contrails visible in the moonlight. It is ten o'clock.

Then, suddenly, a special announcement. Meant for the Dutch population in occupied territory. A cold shiver of tension. This must be something exceptional. A message from the Headquarters of Supreme Allied Command:

'Because the food supplies in occupied Western Holland have been completely exhausted, the Supreme Allied Command has decided to parachute food over the occupied part of Holland. The planes will fly low and drop rations over places where they can be easily collected. Expect these droppings during both day and night. Find shelter if you hear airplanes approaching if you live in an area where droppings can take place. The food packages will not be attached to parachutes so that your life may be endangered if you are hit.'

Fantastic news! Finally food! And the way in which it was to be delivered exceeded the wildest expectations. Low flying aircraft which would drop rations in large numbers – that would be a very impressive operation. Five days of ever-increasing tension follow.

Then, on 29th April, the long-expected announcement is made on the 12 o'clock news broadcast by the BBC. 'Bombers of the Royal Air Force have just taken off from their bases in England to drop food supplies to the Dutch population in enemy-occupied territory.'

There are no words to describe the emotions that 4 million Dutch in the Western part of the country experienced that Sunday afternoon. More than 300 four-engined Lancasters, flying exceptionally low, suddenly filled the western horizon. Motors throbbing, they approached with opened bomb bay doors, filled with large bags of powdered eggs, flour, meat, chocolate and milk powder.

For a moment, the Netherlands holds its breath. The Germans are still in position behind their anti-aircraft guns. Will they fire? That would be mass slaughter. But it remains silent. Then the Dutch go crazy with enthusiasm and relief. No one who experienced this will ever forget those emotional moments.

No one knows how many lives were saved by Operation Manna. But this is certain: just as the children of Israel being led out of the desert by Moses were saved by bread falling from heaven, so did the oppressed and starving Dutch receive aid at a moment when many had given up hope. The RAF policy makers could not have thought of a more appropiate name.

A wave of happiness rolled over occupied Holland. Not only because this was the beginning of the end of starvation. But also because it was now clear that this must certainly mean the end of five years of occupation.

Col. A.P. de Jong,
Royal Netherlands Air Force

Introduction

'Come quickly, they are dropping food . . .!'
With long strides a 17 year old high school pupil rushed downstairs. Ten, fifteen, twenty, thirty enormous low flying British bombers roared over the town.
'Good heavens, look, there they come and there . . . more. Come here, Ma, there are three with the bomb doors open. Oh, if this works out, they are flying over the Flak batteries. If these bloody Huns open fire . . .
I can see the crew. Look, over there inside the cockpit. He is turning his head. He sees us!! The fellow in the rear turret . . . he is waving at us. And over Maassluis I can see more aircraft, all Lancasters. There . . . it says JEC on the fuselage. Oh, look Mrs. Koedijk is crying. Laugh you people, laugh, cheer. Hurray, long live the Tommies. Silly Adje Blauw is standing waving in the street . . . Look at the end of the street. It is crowded with people. This means drudging tomorrow people. All these bags. There are more coming down. What a mass of aircraft. There must be over two hundred and still more are coming. Neighbour, this is the biggest feast we have had for five years. This means the end of all sorrow. Really, the war must be over soon now . . .'
How many Dutch thought and shouted the same words on April 29, 1945? How many of them have also cried? At last. Food – real, genuine, good, tasty, nutritious food. No beet pulp, no more sorrel, no more nettles, no more tulip bulbs, but chocolate, biscuits, 'meat and vegetables', large yellow egg pancakes, tea and fat meat. The elderly people can still remember the smell. Others still love the dark brown chocolate from then. Grown-up men sobbed like little children when they saw and heard the hundreds of

Manna rain . . .

Lancasters approaching from the west shortly after noon on April 29, 1945. Women and girls yelled, waving like mad to the young chaps 'above'. Inside the Lancasters Britons and Canadians, Australians, New Zealanders, Poles and one Dutch airman looked down upon the excited masses below. 'The skipper said to us: God, look at them, the poor buggers. They have turned mad. They just run across the drop zone. If they don't take care they'll be smashed by the food . . .' 'When we flew home the rear gunner said over the intercom: Skip, we'll go back tomorrow, won't we?'

Manna.

Bread from heaven.

'When we flew home across the North Sea it was dead silent inside the Lancaster. Seeing the British coast ahead of us the skipper said: These bloody Jerries, we should line them up against the wall and shoot them all . . .'

Flying Fortress over Vogelenzang Jamboree ground.

Lancaster bomber over Duindigt horse race track.

And they called it Manna . . .

Starvation in Western Netherlands. Usually everyone carried a spoon, just in case one was able to scratch some left-overs from the cooking pots of the Central Kitchens.

When the Netherlands were rudely awakened on May 10th, 1940, still dreaming that neutrality would assure peace, it seemed at first that everything would remain as it always had been. Surely Queen Wilhelmina, Princess Juliana, Prince Bernhard, the two little princesses Beatrix and Irene, the government, everyone had left the country to continue the war from 'elsewhere'. Political parties had disappeared, parliament no longer existed. Rumbling boots stamped in the streets, strange and gutteral voices sang songs that had never been heard before. Rotterdam, Middelburg, Rhenen and other towns in the Netherlands lay in ruins. On the Grebbeberg and in many other places in the country young Dutchmen had been buried after they died defending their homes. They had been the first war casualties since the campaign against the revolutionary Belgians in 1839. But after all, the Germans looked like reasonable decent fellows. They paid cash, behaved correct-

ly and the first Dutch girls could be seen walking holding hands with smart and handsome soldiers. Gradually the situation changed. Some Dutchmen suddenly were treated like garbage because they turned out to be Jewish. The Dutch Nazis, first looked upon compassionately, made themselves hated and feared. Then came the first executions. The first houses were burned down in revenge and the Occupation became more and more difficult. At the beginning of the war aircraft could frequently be heard flying overhead to the east, to come back many hours later. Sometimes a fire could be seen falling from the sky: another British bomber had been shot down. As the war continued the drone of engines increased and waves of RAF bombers became more frequent. In 1943 the Americans

A day's ration in April 1945.
Two potatoes; three slices of bread; some meat substitute and a slice of skim milk cheese.

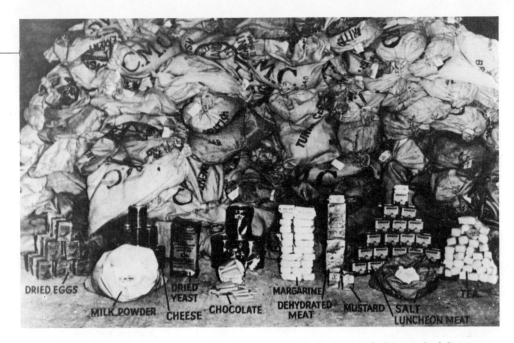

Allied food as it was dropped for the Dutch.

DRIED EGGS MILK POWDER CHEESE DRIED YEAST CHOCOLATE MARGARINE DEHYDRATED MEAT MUSTARD SALT LUNCHEON MEAT TEA

joined in the sorties, so it became a routine: the RAF would come at night, and the Americans on the daylight raids. Sometimes bombs did fall on Dutch towns and people were killed. Seeing and hearing aircraft meant death and destruction, but it also meant something else: each aircraft was a messenger of liberation and salvation from the Occupation forces and their accomplices. In April and May 1945 something incredible happened. Many people thought they would never see liberation, buth then, one morning in April the bombers returned. This time though not at 15,000 or 20,000 feet, but so low that the aircrew could be seen. And . . . the German ack-ack remained silent, the German Luftwaffe stayed on the ground. For almost two weeks hundreds of British and American bombers flew over Western Holland. On board these aircraft were young men, citizens of the British Commonwealth, Poland and the United Stated of America. Unhampered by any German opposition, they crossed the still occupied coast of our country at an extremely low altitude. The German Flak, which had so fiercely fired upon the intruding Lancasters and Flying Fortresses in the prior years remained silent. In the vicinity of large cities, such as The Hague, Rotterdam, Utrecht and Haarlem, the bomb bays opened.

Then the miracle happened: Instead of devastating explosives, food parcels fell to the ground. While thousands of people came out of their houses, cheering and waving, laughing and crying, the enormous aircraft turned and again set course for England, only to return the next day. On that memorable day, Sunday April 29th 1945, Operation Manna began. A bombardment that knows no equal in our history. Manna: In the Netherlands everyone knows the word. In the second book of the Bible, Exodus, we read how Moses received a message from his God during the long journey of the people of Israel through the desert: 'I will rain down bread from heaven for you. Each day the people shall go out and gather a day's supply . . . The Israelites called the food MANNA; it was white like coriander seed and it tasted like a wafer made with honey . . .'

How well this name was chosen in 1945 for the food bombardment. How this food must have tasted like that same wafer made with honey. Nine days later the miracle had become history. In the meantime another miracle had happened: The Netherlands were free, the oppressor had been defeated. At the very last moment our people had been rescued from what some feared: The liberation of corpses.

Forty years after the war, this book wishes to tell how vivid the memories of those people who were part of it still remain; the pilots and their crew members, as well as those who received the food. In this book both groups speak. It recalls the days when the Dutch government in exile appealed for the help of the Allies. You will read about the difficult negotiations with the Germans and how much determination was needed to force them to cooperate passively. One of the Allied officers who was actually present at the negotiations, His Royal Highness Prince Bernhard of the Netherlands, at that time Commander-in-Chief of the Netherlands Forces, will recall the days before the drops.

Forty years after Manna we enjoy freedom and abundance. Compared to developing countries, we live in earth's paradise. In 1945 it was different: people were starving like rats. Sometimes their deaths were concealed to keep their food rations . . .

Images similar to the ones we see today in the Third World, were common in the western part of the Netherlands and the cities of North and South Holland. With this book we intend to honor the ground crews that worked so hard to stow the food in the bomb bays of the Lancasters and the Flying Fortresses. We thank the pilots for whom this was, after the deadly missions to Germany, more than 'flying bloody low without being shot at'.

We remember the crews who packed their own rations as gifts of love thrown down with little parachutes and a small note: 'For the children'.

The postwar generation, the author being one of them, might give Manna a less emotional meaning than those who saw the food come down with their own eyes and those who finally got the chance to bring salvation after so much necessary destruction. But no one will deny that Manna was unique. Unique in design, unique in extent, unique in meaning. Therefore it is good to remember throughout this book and other studies what was done to save our nation from starvation. In addition to this book, other things have been done to keep the memories of the food drops alive. At various times individual pilots and aircrews have been to our country to commemorate Manna. The memory of the food mission has also been kept alive through the issue of a stamp showing Lancaster LS-L for Love of No. 15 Squadron. The idea to write this book was born on May 1, 1983, during a meeting between His Royal Highness Prince Bernhard of the Netherlands and a group of about thirty ex-aircrew members and their wives. With a bit of surprise in his voice, one of the British guests said: 'Strangely enough, the Manna flights were not considered to be operational missions at the time. Therefore little has been done to remember Operation Manna. However seeing how the Dutch have such emotional memories of the Manna-flights, it makes me feel very proud to have been part of it!' For the first time the English guests heard from Prince Bernhard himself about the difficult negotiations and efforts to persuade the Germans to allow the food drops. Many people helped to write this book. I would like to thank some of them. I thank my wife Marjoan, who constantly helped me to collect and arrange the incoming flow of information. Gerdy and Mark-Johan are being thanked for their patience when their parents once again travelled abroad. I thank Peter Groenveld for his skill in reproducing the many hundreds of photographs. Many thanks to Colin and Audrey Hill and to Ron and Julie Stansfield for editing and correcting the English manuscript. I would like to express my thanks to Alan and Lillian Goring, Ken and Joan Ketley, Gordon and Lallie Davies, Pat and Graham Bramble, Peter and Sally Sarll for their hospitality when we stayed in Great Britain. All felt as involved in this Manna-project as they did when they flew their missions of mercy in 1945.

Many thanks to Ted Hine of the Department of Photographs of the Imperial War Museum, to Commander Grefe the assistant navel- and air attaché at the Royal Netherlands Embassy in London, to Group Captain Ian Thompson, OC RAF Scampton and to Air Commodore Probert of the Air Historical Branch MoD/London. Further I would like to thank Ambassador Cumes of Australia, and his successor Ambassador Price, Ambassador Bolt of New Zealand, Ambassador Sir Philip Mansfield of Great Britain and Minister-Counsellor Don Gilchrist of the Canadian Embassy. As 'liasons' between the Manna Committee and their own countries they gave tremendous support helping to collect information and contact former airmen. The chief of the Air Staff RAF Air Chief Marshall Sir Keith Williamson is thanked for his contribution in the preparation of the 1985 reunion. We thank the many contributors of archives in the Nether-

△
Lancaster with stretchers fully loaded.

◁
In the briefing room at Hemswell the crews of 150th and 170th Squadron were briefed about the unique missions they were to fly in the next few days.

Victor Samborski's Lancaster of No. 300 Squadron waiting to be loaded.

lands and abroad, the representatives of Squadron Associations and the Associations of Veterans of the Allied Air Forces. Above all we thank the pilots, gunners, navigators, wireless operators and bomb aimers who reacted spontaneously when we asked them to help us. Many sent us long letters, photographs, flying maps and other documents. These form the majority of the illustrations.

Under the inspiring leadership of Colonel Arie P. de Jong, Royal Netherlands AF, Director of Information at the Department of Defence, an enthusiastic committee was formed. Calling itself the Manna Committee it organized a first reunion of crews of Manna-Squadrons in 1983. Now thanks to the efforts of this Committee a second reunion is being held. This time not only British but also American 'grocers' have come to commemorate the 40th Anniversary of Manna in the midst of their Dutch friends. Apart from Colonel de Jong members of the Committee were: Lieutenant W.J.J. Geneste RN; H.J.L. Hofmeester; W. Latenstein van Voorst; J.

Thoonsen; Mrs. M.G.A. Straathof; Mrs. N. Hanke and J.G. Onderwater. Outside the Committee, many others gave their full-hearted support in making the commemoration a succesful one. The Committee for the National Commemoration of the Liberation gave financial assistance to enable the author to do extensive research. Chief Superintendant C.J. van Dorp, Commanding Officer of the Rotterdam Municipal police allowed me to study the police records. For this I am very grateful.

MANNA/CHOWHOUND should never be forgotten. It saved a part of our population from starvation. It really was Bread from Heaven.

Unfortunately our Allies paid a price for their Missions of Mercy. Several times Lancasters and Flying Fortresses returned to their airfields with bullet holes. Sometimes they were shot at by Germans who could not hide their anger and frustation. On May 7, 1945, two days after the

Germans surrender, a Flying Fortress, 44-8640, crashed into the ice cold water of the North Sea. It is thought to have been hit by fire from German troops concentrated in the IJmuiden area. Eleven crew members lost their lives. Only four bodies were recovered. Seven disappeard without a trace. Two crew members were saved by Air Sea Rescue.

In this book the story of this aircraft and its crew is also told. The names of the killed and missing are:

First Lieutenant Russell H. Cook jr – killed
First Lieutenant Lionel N. Scoorman – killed
Staff Sergeant Gerhard I. Kuper – killed
Technical Sergeant Robert W. Korber – killed
Staff Sergeant Gerald Lane – missing
Staff Sergeant Gen R. McPherson – missing
Staff Sergeant William R. Lankford – missing
Staff Sergeant John W. Keller – missing
Sergeant Joseph R. Repiscah – missing
Private First Class George G. Walters – missing

This book has been dedicated to them. They took off to save us. They did not return to see the results.

Barendrecht, April 1985
Hans Onderwater

A part of the crew of the crashed B-17G. Standing l.-r.: Allen Spance (who didn't fly), McPherson, Korber, Lankford, Keller; Kneeling l.-r.: Anthony Braidic (Dave Condon flew instead of him), Cook, Schwarz (saved), Scoorman.

Prelude

The situation in Holland had changed completely after the advance of the 1st Polish Armoured Division had liberated the entire eastern part of the Netherlands. In the west, the Germans were cut off from their own country, making the troops in that area of little importance in terms of the campaign of Montgomery's forces. What mattered now was to destroy the main German armies and thus end the war. All lands held by Hitler's soldiers, including 'Fortress Holland' would thereby be liberated all at once. But, the fact that the Dutch people inside the fortress were all in danger of starvation put a different face on the matter. It was vital to relieve them at the earliest practical moment, and the Dutch Government in exile in London lost no opportunity to keep this fact before its allies. And yet the problem was not a matter of whether the necessary military resources could be spared from the main campaign for the liberation of the area, but rather that a Liberation by force would involve fierce fighting, and this in turn would bring ruin to many Dutch cities and towns. And, more seriously, it might result in the Germans opening the dikes and ruining the low-lying countryside between the sea and Utrecht. The background of this dilemma is a long and melancholy story. When the Germans first occupied Holland they made some friendly gestures to the population. But soon the people showed the Germans that they considered them to be enemies. By early 1941 the German Reichskommissar, the Austrian Arthur Seyss-Inquart, already knew that he could not count on a submissive Dutch attitude. In London, the Dutch Government in exile inspired by Queen Wilhelmina, fanned the spirit of revolution and resistance. First the Germans ran into trouble when they started their policy of humiliation of the Dutch Jews. The Dutch, not willing to agree, went on strike. The Germans answered with bloodshed. In May 1943, again strikes broke out when the Dutch ex-POW's were ordered to report for transportation back to POW camps in Germany. Again the German reaction was cruel and ruthless. When Allied airborne forces later attempted the landings near Arnhem in September 1944 the Dutch Government called a general railway strike throughout the country. In retaliation Seyss-Inquart imposed an embargo on food supplies for urban western areas from the eastern agricultural districts. Food stocks in the densely populated west had already been reduced by German order and there was not enough left to help the people through the winter. There also was a shortage of coal. These developments occurred when the Allies were making a supreme effort to cross the Rhine and win the war before the end of the year. If this would have been possible, the Dutch could have been helped just in time. Alas, these hopes were disappointed. The Dutch authorities in London observed all this with growing concern. On October 8th 1944 Queen Wilhelmina appealed to President Roosevelt for help. He answered that everything would be done to help, but only after the liberation.

As the weeks passed Dutch pressure for a political solution to the growing crisis increased.

*The credentials of
Air Commodore
Geddes.*

CREDENTIAL FOR A MILITARY PARTY IN HOLLAND
CONCERNING SUPPLY OF FOOD TO THE DUTCH

To whom it may concern.

No. 25011 AIR COMMODORE ANDREW JAMES WRAY GEDDES,
D.S.O., O.B.E., ROYAL AIR FORCE, is hereby accredited as
representative of the AIR OFFICER COMMANDING-IN-CHIEF, SECOND
TACTICAL AIR FORCE, on the instruction of the SUPREME COMMANDER,
ALLIED EXPEDITIONARY FORCES, to take part in the discussion
to determine the method by which the DUTCH are to be supplied
with food in the immediate future.

AIR COMMODORE GEDDES will be the Air representative
in the party to be headed by MAJOR GENERAL SIR FRANCIS DE GUINGAND,
K.B.E., C.B.E., D.S.O., to discuss these arrangements with enemy
representatives on 29th April 1945 in enemy territory.

Signed ....
Air Marshal,
Air Officer Commanding-in-Chief,
SECOND TACTICAL AIR FORCE, R.A.F.

28th April, 1945.

SHAEF had in fact prepared a plan in October 1944. This divided the Netherlands into three main areas: 'A', the part south of the Waal-river; 'B', the area west of the river IJssel; and 'C' the remainder east of the IJssel. The 'B' -area was subdivided into 'B-1' and 'B-2', east and west, respectively, of a line from Hilversum through Utrecht to Tiel.

The 'B-2' area constituted the chief problem. It was calculated that 2,000 tons of food would be necessary to daily feed 3,600,000 people in the B-2 area. For this reason the 21st Army Group was instructed to establish stockpiles. Near the town of Oss a large stockpile of 30,000 tons was waiting to be distributed. In mid-January 1945, after the Battle of the Bulge and after a very severe winter in western Holland, the mounting crisis was such that Queen Wilhelmina addressed identical notes to King George VI, President Roosevelt and Winston Churchill. In her letter Her Majesty wrote with great anxiety:

'Conditions have at present become so desperate that it is abundantly clear that if a major catastrophe, the like of which

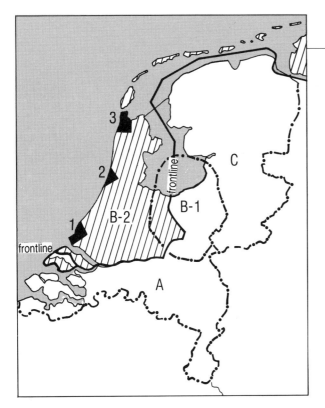

The Netherlands prior to Operation Manna/Chowhound.

German occupied ◿◿◿◿ ▲ *'Sperrgebiet'*

Restricted area: 1. Hook of Holland
2. IJmuiden
3. Den Helder

A area: liberated in 1944

B-1 area: liberated in April 1945

B-2 area: starvation area

C area: liberated in April 1945

has not been seen in western Europe since the Middle Ages, is to be avoided in Holland something drastic has to be done now, that is to say before and not after the liberation of the rest of the country!'

For months efforts had been in progress to bring relief to occupied Holland through the Swedish and the International Red Cross. It had little result. At the end of January two small Swedish ships landed 3,200 tons at Delfzijl. It took nearly two weeks to reach Amsterdam. Another vessel, operated by the International Red Cross, eventually delivered additional supplies in early

March. The Germans brought in 2,600 tons of rye from Oldenburg. But these measures fell far short of requirements.

At the end of March a Red Cross delegate, who had supervised the distribution of these supplies, reported:

> 'The physical conditions of the western provinces having reduced the inhabitants almost to a primitive state, they are obliged in the struggle for existence, to engage in the black market, in usury and even in theft. Some eat flower bulbs. The bombed houses are pilaged and looted of all combustible material. The trees in the gardens are cut and carried away by night. Horses killed by bombardments are immediately cut up by passers-by. The bread wagons in the cities can only circulate under police protection because if not protected they will be attacked and plundered.'

The caloric content had fallen to 500. The death rate was nearly double to that for equivalent periods in 1944. At the end of 1944 the Germans began to undermine the dike of the Wieringermeer Polder, one of the newest polders. It was obvious that the Germans would not hesitate to flood other parts of the country. It was also obvious that something had to be done immediately. On March 27th, 1945 General Dwight D. Eisenhower, Supreme Commander of the Allied Forces in Europe, informed the Combined Chiefs of Staff that Holland would suffer heavily if the Allied Forces went in to attack and liberate the people. Therefore 'Ike' considered it militarily inadvisable to undertake operations west of Utrecht as long as the Germans maintained cohesive resistance and added:

> 'Suggest you make clear to the Royal Netherlands Government the great cost of Dutch lives and property.'

In the meantime the British Air Ministry, in consultation with SHAEF, prepared the plan to

bring supplies into the Netherlands by air. It calculated that the Allied air forces could deliver 2,200 tons of food daily. The plan was based on the assumption that no German opposition would be encountered. The Plan carried the name PLACKET-C.

On March 15th, 1945 Group Captain W.D. Macpherson prepared a secret minute entitled 'Relief food for the Dutch; 38 Group Carrying Capacity'. The minute read:

> 'At present 1,000,000 ration packets have been released for free dropping. These rations weigh 1,900,000 lbs.
>
> 38 Group aircraft can at present average 4,000 lbs per aircraft for free dropping, but it is expected shortly to increase the load to 5,000 lbs or more.
>
> Taking 5,000 lbs as the average load, the aircraft sorties required to drop 1,900,000 lbs amount to 380.
>
> Assuming that all serviceable aircraft of 38 Group are allocated to drop these supplies it should be possible to provide 200 aircrafts. Therefore the 1,000,000 packets can be dropped in two sorties. If 38 Group is to operate more than two sorties on this task, the figure of 200 aircraft should not be assumed owing to other commitments and Stirling unserviceability.'

Two factors now operated to bring a solution to the intolerable situation: the Allied leaders' real-

At the end of January 1945 the Swedish vessel 'Hallaren' brought food to our country.

ization that further delay would be disastrous and the willingness of the German authorities – in the sinister person of the Austrian Arthur Seyss-Inquart – to negotiate. On March 21th, a week before General Eisenhower made it clear that no immediate attack in a westerly direction was possible, it was decided to arrange for a meeting at the Holland District Command Headquarters on Wednesday March 28th at 1430 hours. Participating representatives came from the military as well from the civil servants of the British Foreign Office. The purpose of the conference was to discuss and draw up a Directive to implement the request of Holland District Command; that is, to supply food to the Dutch population by air both by dropping and landing bulk supply at existing airfields in Holland. On March 30th, the meeting took place at the HQ of General Galloway of West Holland District Command to discuss the operation. Representatives of SHAEF Netherlands, CATOR, 21st Army Group, War Office, RAF and Special Forces HQ were present. It was stated at that conference that SHAEF had ordered the release of one million POW rations for distribution to the Dutch population, together with another two million rations, provided that the latter were replaceable. The representative of the War Office pointed out that the SHAEF Directive was

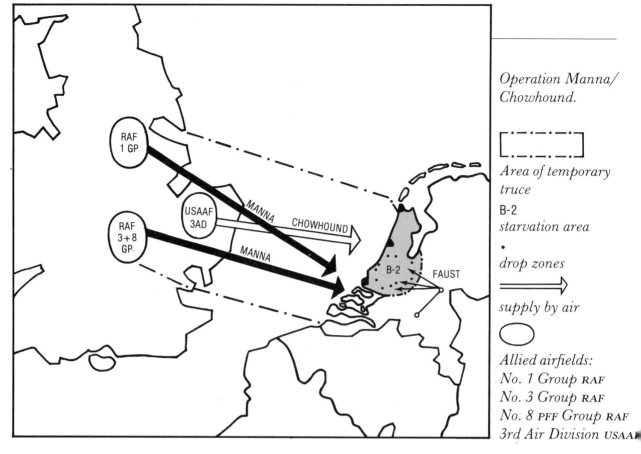

*Operation Manna/
Chowhound.*

*Area of temporary
truce*

B-2
starvation area

•

drop zones

⟹

supply by air

◯

Allied airfields:
No. 1 Group RAF
No. 3 Group RAF
No. 8 PFF *Group* RAF
3rd Air Division USAAF

not quite clear on this point in that, according to his information, replacements of the latter two million rations would not be available for six weeks. The War Office representative was requested to obtain clarification on this point and it was generally anticipated at the meeting that, in fact, the total three million rations would be made available for PLACKET-C, especially since conditions were not unsatisfactory in those POW camps already liberated by the Allied Armies. It was understood that the three million rations were part of a total of eleven million rations originally allocated to supply to POW's. No. 38 Group was requested to carry out the dropping, and it was understood that they would need all of the 200 aircraft available. Each aircraft was to carry out two sorties daily, making a total of 400 sorties. The aircraft would be Halifaxes and Stirlings, with an average load of 2,5 tons.

During the conference all participants heard with great interest that the Dutch Resistance would be able to handle the reception and distribution of the food. But it was soon understood from Dutch authorities that PLACKET-C was bound to fail because there would be no certainty that the food would reach the people. The Germans, not being involved in the planning, most certainly would confiscate the food and use it for themselves. Black marketeers would be able to make a lot of money on any food that they would get a hold of. Riots and fights among starving Dutch could cause many casualties. To assure a fair distribution it would be absolutely necessary to negotiate directly with the occupation authorities. Without the Germans any attempt to supply food would be a dissipation of food, aircraft and manpower.

On April 10th, 1945 Sir Winston Churchill wrote to President Roosevelt: 'I fear we may soon be in the presence of a tragedy' and proposed a delivery of supplies by sea from areas under the military control of the Allies. Two days later, on April 12th Franklin D. Roosevelt died. Upon hearing the news the vile German Minister of Propaganda Joseph Goebbels told Hitler that he received his long-awaited 'Indication from Providence' . . .

In the meantime in Brabant contact had been made between the Allies and Dutch representatives from the Occupied Territory. On behalf of the Committee of 'Vertrouwensmannen' or 'The Trusted' two brave man, Van der Gaag and Neher, crossed the lines and arrived in the South. After having informed Prince Berhard of the situation, they left for London to tell Dutch Prime Minister Gerbrandy about the developments in that part of the Netherlands still under German control. They told Gerbrandy that the Germans would be willing to negotiate if certain conditions were accepted. The Germans also promised to stop further destructions, executions and all actions against the Resistance as well as to give political prisoners better treatment. In the opinion of the Dutch government, these German proposals were worth consideration. On April 14th, 1945 Prince Bernhard travelled to Reims in order to discuss the Allied answer with General Eisenhower.

In London, Gerbrandy consulted with Churchill. The British leader however did not feel like negotiating with an enemy already on its knees. Thanks to mediation of the South African Prime Minister Fieldmarshal Smuts however, the British Premier allowed direct negotiations with the Germans. It was not until April 24th that the governments of the United States, Great Britain and the Soviet Union finally allowed Eisenhower to contact Seyss-Inquart, the German governor of Occupied Holland.

That same day people listening to Allied-operated Radio Luxemburg heard that food drops were about to be started:

'German authority is restricted to only a few pockets of resistance in Germany. To alleviate the sufferings of the Dutch population during the final phase of the fighting the Allied Supreme Commander decrees that the Dutch civilian population is to be supplied with food dropped by parachutes. A great number of aircraft of all types will be employed by day and night to carry these foodstuffs. These aircraft are not being used for purposes of war but serve to bring aid to a destitute population.'

The message ended with precise directions to be followed by the Germans. In order to force the Germans to cooperate, they were told that the only way to assure themselves of POW-status was to obey completely. Acts of sabotage would be considered a war crime and any Germans interfering with the Allied effort would be treated as war criminals. Furthermore, the announcer said that the announcement would be repeated in Dutch and at dictation speed in German that same day at 2350 hours.

The next day at 2000 hours the well known voice of 'The Rotterdammer', the alias of H. J. van den Broek, could be heard on Radio Resurgent Netherlands. He too prepared the Dutch for the coming food supply missions.

The Germans, not at all impressed and rather angry since all arrangements had been made without consulting them, answered the Allied challenge that same evening through German-controlled Radio Hilversum in Occupied Holland.

'As far as we know, the population in the provinces of North and South Holland and in Utrecht amounts to 5 million people. If the Allies intend to supply food for 10 million people daily, an air fleet will be necessary which will be busy day and night. As humanitarian feelings were never typical of Allied methods of waging war, this Anglo-American action raises suspicions.

On 19th April 1945 at 17.50 hrs, Squadron Leader W. Gorrie took off from RAF Witchford (No. 115 Squadron) in order to demonstrate the drop procedure to be used to Marshal of the RAF

Date	Hour	Aircraft Type and No.	Pilot	Duty	REMARKS (Including results of bombing, gunnery, exercises, et
19.4.45	17.58	LANCASTE I. A. PA 181.	S/L GORRIE	NAVIGATOR.	SPECIAL DUTY DEMONSTRATION for MARSHAL OF RAF. LORD TRENCHARD. 0.15 min.
		LANCASTER I.			

Lord Trenchard and other dignitaries. This test flight took only 15 minutes as can be seen from F/L Armitage's log book.

The German Military Commander in the Netherlands agrees in principle with General Eisenhower's plan to supply food to the Occupied Netherlands, but does not approve of the means suggested as pilots would be able to observe his defence works.'

Of course there was not a single object of defence that had escaped the eyes of Allied cameras flown over Holland in Mosquitoes and Spitfires each day. Photograph after photograph had been made of tank traps, trenches, pillboxes and batteries. Still the Allies had to put up with the German refusal:

'As the heavy bombers which were to have dropped the food would be unarmed and would fly at an extremely low level they would be very vulnerable to AA-fire which the Germans would undoubtedly use.'

For the Dutch it was a bitter disappointment. The hope for quick help vanished. ANEP-ANETA reported that the Allies were now busy trying to think of another possibility to send help. It did not give the Dutch much comfort. Now that it had been proven how a too-quickly-given promise affected the morale of the besieged people, all

Allied radio correspondents were told not to give any false hope in the matter of food supply flights.

The same day however a message was sent from the Netherlands to London. It was a message from Colonel Koot, the Commander of the Interior Forces (The Resistance) in Fortress Holland. Seyss-Inquart, like Himmler, was under the impression that he could come to a separate peace with the Western Allies, and said that he was prepared to accept proposals with reference to food aid.

Eisenhower, in the meantime, ordered the drops to start on April 27, whatever the German reaction would be. Prince Bernhard came to meet the German Supreme Commander Blaskowitz by promoting Colonel Koot to Major-General over the telephone. Now the Colonel-General no lon-

The Mosquitoes photographed the drop fields and functioned as target indicators.

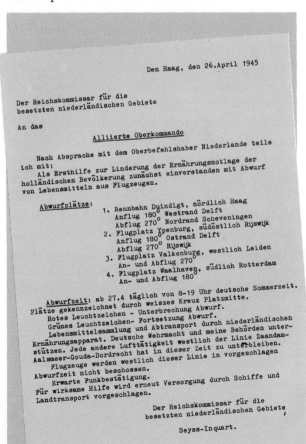

ger had to talk with a simple Dutch Colonel. A week before the date set by Eisenhower in England, the necessary preparatory work had been done to begin the food drops. Already in February the RAF had flown test drops at Netheravon airfield and had proven that the dropping of food in sacks would be quite possible if the pilots kept a fixed airspeed, altitude and position of flaps. The scientists however thought this solution was too simple. They could not believe that food packed in burlap sacks would survive a 300 foot free fall. Besides that they decided it would be impossible to drop the load at a right spot.

On 26 April Seyss-Inquart, the German Governor of the Occupied Western part of the Netherlands, finally agreed that the fastest way to save the Dutch was to send food supplies by air.

A story was told that the RAF suggested a demonstration. This was done. The sacks came down almost on the feet of the experts. One thing went wrong however. When dropped at the speed and altitude suggested by the 'Back Room Boys' the sacks landed right in front of the experts. They had been filled with a mixture of soot and chalk; the RAF had made its point . . .

Sadly enough bad weather prevented the Lancasters from taking off on the 27th of April. Again all hope seemed to have vanished. On April 28th it was finally possible to start the operation. The two opposing parties would meet in the little village of Achterveld, not very far from Amersfoort. As a token of good will the Allies informed the Germans that all shooting would stop from Saturday morning 0800 hours April 28, till Sunday morning April 29th, 0800 hours. An unreal silence came over the lines. The Germans, still not certain that help and not bombs would come, decided to prepare themselves for landings of parachutists, aircraft and weapons.

That morning the inhabitants of Achterveld were surprised when they suddenly saw all kinds of Allied vehicles moving through the village. The people were told to stay inside their houses. The Roman Catholic Saint Joseph Elementary School was surrounded by Allied soldiers. High ranking Canadian and British officers were seen walking on the school grounds.

Among these officers was an Air Commodore of the RAF. His name was Andrew Geddes. That same morning he had accompanied Montgomery's Chief of Staff, Sir Francis De Guingand, to Achterveld. Air Commodore Geddes being 'Air Commodore Operations and Plans' at the Headquarters of the Second Tactical Air Force of the RAF had been told to establish as many drop zones as possible. Further he would have to overcome any German objections and convince them that it would be very 'unhealthy' to interfere in the operation to come. In his briefcase he

Air Commodore Andrew Wray Geddes CBE, DSO, Legion of Merit (USA), RAF (retd). In 1945, Air Commodore Operations and Plans, Headquarters 2nd Tactical Air Force RAF.

carried a list of no less than 104 possible areas. Andrew Geddes came well prepared. He also had the difficult job of writing an agreement to assure an unhampered drop of all foodstuffs. He had long before written down that the Germans would be escorted to Achterveld after having crossed their own first lines and then being picked up by Canadian soldiers. They were to be taken to Achterveld blindfolded. Later one of the Germans would complain about this. He too expressed his anger for being called 'Fritz' by one of the Canadian soldiers.

In Occupied Holland meanwhile the people waited for the food with great anxiety. On 26th April a 17 year old boy from Rotterdam by the name of Kees den Haan, wrote in his diary:

> 'At six in the morning I was queuing for Red Cross bread and butter. At seven my mother took my place. At eight we finally got it. There are German police driving through town. They wear steel helmets. I will not go out today. Strange rumours are heard.'

The next day he wrote again and wondered how

long the war would continue. Kees of course knew nothing about the negotiations at Achterveld. In this village, in the meantime, a lot of movement was noticed. Despatch riders came and went, a Jeep stopped in front of the school. A few minutes later a small convoy arrived. German officers came out of Allied cars. After their blindfolds had been removed they slowly walked towards the school surrounded by Allied soldiers. Upon arrival in the school the Germans expected a hearty welcome from their Allied adversaries. However they were wrong indeed. When they made an attempt to shake hands they received a cold military salute in return.

De Guingand presided over the first meeting. Other Allied participants were a representative of Eisenhower, a Russian officer and other military experts on transport matters and food supplies.

In 1984 Air Commodore Geddes gave a vivid description of the German delegates:

'The German delegation consisted of four persons. Reichsrichter Dr. Ernst Schwebel, Dr. Plutzar, Hauptmann Dr. Stoeckle and Oberleutnant Von Massow. Schwebel was a Junker-type of German officer with an enormous strawberrylike red nose and scars of duelling. Dr. Plutzar was a civil servant and produced reference papers while the Reichsrichter spoke. Schwebel did not speak any English, but Plutzar spoke English fluently. At times he corrected the interpreter's translations when he felt that the meaning of the British speech had not been translated correctly to Schwebel. Stoeckle was the only German delegate who gave the Nazi salute. He wore epaulets with the figures '39' on it and looked a typical Nazi. Oberleutnant Von Massow spoke perfect English and took detailed notes of the conversations.'

When the meeting started General De Guingand told the German delegates the object of the meeting; which was to come to an agreement as to how the Allies could best help the Dutch (in view of the fact that the Germans were not in a position to do so) by way of bringing food into the country, distributing it within Holland and assisting the Dutch medically. De Guingand also stated that he was authorized to speak on behalf of the Supreme Commander, General Eisenhower, concerning a proposal put forward by Reichskommissar Seyss-Inquart for a truce.

The German delegates arrived on 30th April in Canadian staff cars in Achterveld.

On the airfields of Nos. 1 and 3 Groups, the military men literally worked day and night to load the Lancasters.

He suggested that the matter should be left to the end of the meeting.

Schwebel, who was the spokesman for Seyss-Inquart, said that his terms of reference did not include making detailed arrangements for the feeding of the Dutch. He had been sent by the Reichskommissar to make arrangements whereby Seyss-Inquart could meet General Eisenhower, or a representative of the Supreme Commander of the Allied Armies at some agreed place on Monday, April 30th, each accompanied by a delegation of experts. He indicated he was not in a position to make any agreement on behalf of Seyss-Inquart, except as far as arranging for the next meeting was concerned.

General De Guingand then went through his proposals so that the German delegates should arrive on Monday April 30th with proper experts able to effect an agreement and make the necessary decisions so that no further delays should occur in feeding the Dutch. As he came to each method of providing food for the Dutch

population, he called upon the required experts to outline the British proposals; the expert for Air Supply being Air Commodore Geddes, the expert for Inland Water Transport and Road Transport being Major-General Galloway and the expert for Transport by Sea being Captain Jeffreys RN.

Prince Bernhard of the Netherlands also advised General De Guingand on the Dutch representatives to participate in the next meeting. The other experts would include Colonel Poole on tonnages available and Colonel Zenkovitch on the interests of the Soviet government and in particular the feeding of Russian displaced persons, POW's and internees. Brigadier Williams would act as Secretary to the Meeting. General De Guingand then detailed the points on which decisions would have to be taken at the meeting of April 30th. It was agreed that the following meeting would be held at 1300 hours (German Summer Time) on April 30th, 1945 with Lieutenant General Bedell Smith, Chief of Staff to General Eisenhower, leading the delegation. German Army, Air Force and Naval representatives would form part of the German delegation. The Dutch director of Food, Ir. Louwes, would accompany the German delegates. General Crerar, the Commander of the First Canadian Army, would be present if possible. While these negotiations were taking place, the 'best operations ever flown' were about to begin.

The next day, April 29th, hundreds of Dutch people in cellars, attics and some hiding behind cupboards listened to the voice of freedom. At 0800 hours Radio Resurgent Netherlands broke the spell. With a special announcement by the Allied Supreme Commander the great news was told. Aircraft would come to drop coloured flares. A little later other airplanes should drop the food. At 1210 hours the long awaited message came through the radio:

'...Special announcement. A few minutes ago the BBC reported that the first aircraft carrying food for Occupied Holland have left...' Even before the negotiations had been concluded the Allies had made a final decision. Hundreds of people left their houses to see the miracle with their very own eyes. Operation Manna had begun!

It wil be clear to the reader what tremendous risk the RAF took. No agreement had yet been signed when the first Lancasters approached Occupied Holland. At an extremely low altitude of 150-1,000 feet the large four-engined bombers would have been an easy prey for the many anti-aircraft guns the Germans could still deploy in the besieged Fortress Holland. Even if the Germans had opened fire and killed hundreds of young Britons and other Allies, they would have had the right to do so. The responsible commanders of the RAF knew the risk they took, knew the terrible tragedy that could have happened over Holland if the Germans had opened fire. Above all they knew that any German reaction would be legitimate. The commanders knew it; so did the pilots and their crew members...

Aerial view of the church of Brouwershaven on 29 April 1945.

God, oh God, there they come!

The Germans expected the droppings to begin the moment their delegates entered Achterveld. Therefore they had placed anti-aircraft guns around the drop zones the Allies had chosen. German police and members of the SD, the infamous secret police, had arrived there to control the supplies and see if between the foodstuffs any weapons, explosives and other materials for sabotage had been hidden. At Ypenburg airfield the SS-general Schöngarth, accompanied by the chief of the secret police, Mundt, and several helpers of the Dutch Director-General for Food distribution, Louwes, had come to witness the arrival of the Lancasters. The sky had remained empty; again bad weather had spoiled everything.

On April 28th at 2200 hours Radio Resurgent Netherlands reported that the negotiations at Achterveld had been concluded successfully. It was not really true. Dr. Schwebel, the representative of Seyss-Inquart, being nothing more than the governor's messenger-boy had only taken the Allied proposals with him.

At several airfields in England great consternation arose when the crews heard that Manna was 'on'. In the briefing rooms where the crews were usually informed about the targets that had to be attacked and where more and more very young crews took the place of the men who had been killed or taken prisoner, cries of bewilderment were heard.

'Today we will fly to Holland to drop food. Our altitude over the target will be 500 feet. The Germans have opened corridors over the area to let us through. There will be no shooting on both sides.'

'What? My God, who has gone crazy? Ridicu-

The crew of Lancaster IQ-E 'Eazie Duzzit' of No. 150 Squadron, better known as 'Bramble's Shambles'. Standing from left to right: Sgt McGrath (rear gunner), Sgt Card (navigator), F/o Bramble (pilot), Sgt Gaulton (flight engineer), Flt/Sgt Verdon (bomb aimer) and Sgt Ofley (mid-upper gunner). Kneeling 'Smokey', one of the ground crew members and Sgt Old (wireless operator).

lous, bloody nonsense, that is what it is!'

Others remained silent, probably wondering why they were being sent on such a mission at a time when everyone knew that Jerry was about to be finished off once and for all.

A derisive laughter went up in the briefing room at RAF Hemswell. Crews of Nos. 150 and 170 Squadron listened with growing horror to William Jones, the Intelligence Officer.

'Since when do we trust the bloody Hun? Have we not learned enough in Munich?' wondered Flying Officer Graham Bramble. Many times he had taken his crew over Germany. They had been very lucky indeed. With his crew he had formed an international team of airmen; an Australian, an Englishman, a Welshman, a Scotsman, a Canadian, a Cockney and a genuine subject of the Irish Republic of whom everyone wondered whether he would return to base every time he went on leave to Eire. Graham Bramble who sometimes was a bit of a 'bad lad', had had his fair share of troubles with the Hun as well as with his CO. Some people called him the most experienced orderly officer. Once while being detailed to tow the drogue and as such practically being a target for the other gunners who would empty their .30 guns at the drogue, he had dropped the line of the drogue on the large white 'T' at the base and destroyed it completely.

And now he had to fly this food mission at a time when the war had almost being been finished by the Allied armies. Bramble believed that April 1945 was not the right date to die, especially while being defenceless at 500 feet over enemy territory. He was not the only pilot with mixed feelings about Manna.

When the green light was given, no less than 246 Lancasters took off for Holland. Eighteen Mosquitoes went in first. They were to mark the drop zones. The crews were all tense and, as some would remember, their hearts were thumping and their mouths were dry.

The approach of the bombers brought waves of emotion and expectation in Occupied Holland. A 17 your old high school pupil from Vlaardingen, Arie de Jong, wrote in his diary later that day:

'1300 hours, April 29th, great tension. Everybody is standing in the street looking to the West. The entire world knows it. At approximately 10,000 feet some Mosquito scouts fly over. 1310 hours till 1500 hours. They fly over at 70 to 160 feet making a hellish sound crossing the Nieuwe Waterweg into the direction Vlaardingen. Some aircraft turn North direction Delft and The Hague. Others head for Rotterdam. The German Flak remains silent. Still it was a bit exciting; how would this end? One could see the gunners waving in their turrets. A marvellous sight. One Lancaster roared over the town at 70 feet. I saw the aircraft tacking between church steeples and drop its bags in the South. Later on many returning aircraft flying very low took part in this fantastic spectacle. Everywhere we looked, bombers could be seen. No one remained inside and everybody dared to wave cloths and flags. What a feast!

Pictures were made of a Lancaster. They used the old paper film for it. I counted more than 200 aircraft. At about three o'clock the last aircraft were again heading for the sea. Everyone is excited with joy. The war must be over soon now.'

Arie de Jong's first taste of the heavenly food was a memorable one. When a Lancaster dropped a sack near Vlaardingen, he and other boys rushed to the spot where they expected the food to come down. It turned out to be a yellow powder. The boys started to gorge themselves on it. It was egg powder. Coughing and blowing yellow clouds the boys threw up.

That first day, April 29th, 239 of 246 Lancasters dropped over 500 tons of food at four designated dropping areas; Waalhaven airfield, Ypenburg airfield, Duindigt race track and Valkenburg airfield. Some Lancasters dropped food way outside the agreed area. Food also fell near Haamstede, on the island of Schouwen-Duiveland, where the first bombers had entered hostile airspace that afternoon.

The Nazi-burgomaster of Haamstede, J.P.C. Boot made precise reports in his diary each day. On April 28th he had been informed about the droppings by the German Island Commandant Oberleutnant Hinricher. The flight path of the bombers would come very close to his village with Schouwen-Duiveland and Goeree-Overflakkee as the southern and northern boundaries of the corridor. On April 29th, burgomaster Boot wrote:

'Sunday April 29th. During the morning there was some snow. It was chilly. Between approximately 1440 and 1445 a number of four-engined bombers flew low over the village. They were aircraft coming back from the food drops. One of the aircraft, according to eye-witnesses, with one of its four engines stopped, made a turn and dropped a number of parcels (about 60) near 'Gadra' house. This was not according to the agreement, for Schouwen had not been mentioned as one of the dropping areas and no fields had been prepared for the purpose. One of the policemen who saw it happen came to me and informed me about it. He also told me that people living in the neighbourhood of the drop were busy dragging the parcels away. After consulting councillor Den Boer, who too was an eyewitness, I issued the message that alle parcels had to be taken to the councillor's since they were meant for the starving people of Rotterdam. The drop here must have been a misunderstanding. Apart from some exceptions people obeyed the orders. According to what has been written on the outside of the boxes the parcels contain: flour, meat, vegetables, soup, yeast, tea, chocolate.

That same afternoon I discussed the matter with Island Commandant Lieutenant Hinricher. He agreed with me that the good were meant for Rotterdam and promised to provide me with means of transportation. He wished to have

29 April 1945. A Lancaster over the Pietermanstraat, near the Lange Hilleweg in Rotterdam.

some people from the Westhoek to accompany the transport to keep things under control. It was not difficult to find volunteers since many villagers have friends or relatives in Rotterdam.'

In Rotterdam great enthusiasm and happiness was evident when the first Lancasters roared over the town after having dropped their load at Waalhaven aerodrome. Mr.W.J. van Rijn was one of the people who will never forget this day; it was his wife's birthday as well. When the first Lancasters flew over very low at 1300 hours even German soldiers watched the bombers with their mouths wide open. One young German private got such a shock that he ran away in terror.

One of the many hundreds of aircrew members who came to our country that memorable April 29th was a civilian. He was H. George Franks, who worked at ANP, the Dutch press agency in London. During the days before the drops he had travelled to many airfields and informed the crews about the sufferings of the Dutch. Thus he had tried to convince the crews how important their missions would be. Now he had been given permission to accompany a crew. After a hasty breakfast, Franks climbed into a Lancaster at approximately noon. His skipper was Flight Lieutenant Chedwell. Half an hour later the bomber took of.

For the first time Franks saw with his own eyes the floodings caused when the German blew holes in the dikes.

'It was 1342 hours and at that time we saw the first signs of habitation. Below us were four barges tied up to a canal bank. From these barges suddenly half a dozen men emerged waving like mad at us with a Dutch flag. Near Rotterdam we turned north and headed for The Hague, along the route prescribed by the Germans. In the field, on the roads and even in the gardens of the sad little houses everyone seemed to be waving frantically with flags, tablecloths of anything they had been able to grab. Two man standing next to two German soldiers at a street corner suddenly took off their jackets and waved at us. On the rooftop of what seemed to be a nunnery we saw a few nuns who had taken of their white-winged hats to join in the welcome. The skipper allowed me to drop the food. Within a few seconds it seemed that a giant's hand was fluttering confetti over the Hague. The smoke signals of the markers dropped by the Pathfinders earlier were clearly visible in the target area.'

The first days drops had been a miraculous success. Even though the Germans had been ordered only to open fire if the bombers left the corridor, several Lancasters returned with bullet holes. General Eisenhower had a message sent to Seyss-Inquart immediately:

'Your troops firing small arms at our aircraft. Please ensure this ceases immediately.'

The same day, Franks informed the Dutch Prime Minister Gerbrandy about the success of the drops. One of Gerbrandy's first questions was: 'Has the Peace Palace survived?' Apparently he had not been convinced that the British precision attack at the Central Population Administration Centre had been as successful as he had been informed. The next day the bombers would come back. That same day a second meeting was to take place between the Germans and the Allies at Achterveld. As demanded by General De Guingand, this time, the Germans sent delegates who were able to make decisions. As said, Air Commodore Geddes was to establish the drop zones. On April 29th he had already written a concept for the agreement to be signed.

Negotiations

During an interview he gave the author at his home in East Sussex Air Commodore Andrew J.W. Geddes, now 79 years old but still very vital, told how he remembered the second meeting between the Allies and the Germans on April 30th, 1945.

'...General Bedell Smith, the Chief of Staff of General Eisenhower presided over the meeting. Others present were HRH Prince Bernhard and his chief of staff, Colonel Van Houten. I came with Freddie de Guingand. I recall a Russian General Suslaporov and many other Allied officers, NCO's and soldiers walking about. Very soon the people in Achterveld found out that Prince Bernhard had arrived. They greeted him as an old and very dear friend. "How is the Princess, how are the little princesses?" These were questions he had to answer. I was near HRH when a lady and her two daughters presented the Prince with flowers. The Prince had made sure that his car had been parked in a very visible place. This car had been the official car of Seyss-Inquart and still carried the German license plate "RK-1". White stars had been painted on the sides and the engine hood, but for the rest it still was very much the car of Reichskommissar Seyss-Inquart.

When the Germans were taken to the meeting the civilian people began showing their disapproval and shouted and yelled. As expected the car with Seyss-Inquart stopped next to the one now belonging to Prince Bernhard. When Seyss-Inquart saw his former vehicle, his mouth fell wide open and it clearly showed that he was very, very annoyed by the whole affair.

We recognized several Germans from photographs we had of them. Again there was Schwebel with his interpreters Plutzar and Von Massow. I was quite sure that Von Massow was an intelligence officer. Further I saw General Plocher, Major Groebe and other officers of the German Air Force and Navy. An officer of West Holland District was also present. Rear Admiral Faulkner acted as an expert on naval matters. The Germans were accompanied by Dutch experts who had come with them from occupied

HRH Prince Bernhard arrived in style; he came in the car that once belonged to Seyss-Inquart.

territory. I recall they insisted on being treated as a separate delegation. We knew they were "good" Dutchmen. I am sure Prince Bernhard would not have accepted them if they had been traitors or collaborators with the Germans. All in all it was an emotional situation. These people were still under occupation and now suddenly stood face to face with their liberators. The presence of Prince Bernhard meant an awful lot to them. All these years they had been separated form their Queen and tried to cooperate with the Germans even though they hated them so much. They all had tears in their eyes when they were met by the Prince who shook hands and talked with them.'

They were S.L. Louwes, the Secretary-General for Food distribution, Dr. M.J.L. Dols and Messrs. J.J. Oyevaar, H.J. v.d. Roemer, C.J. van Schelle, H.H. Wemmers and C. Banning. Swedish citizens were present as observers.

This April 30th in 1945 would be the only day in his life that HRH Prince Bernhard completely forgot the birthday of his wife. While interviewed by Dutch television during a 1983 visit of former RAF aircrew, all of them former participants of the 'RAF-Grocery-Run', HRH remembered:

'I had arrived in Seyss-Inquart's car. I stood leaning against his car when he arrived. He did not like that very much. Seyss-Inquart was accompanied by Dutch officials, all experts on matters of food and transport. We first greeted our fellow-countrymen very cordially and gave them cigarettes and food. The Germans were put in a separate room and did not get anything. We were very busy that day and so emotionally involved in the things going on that I completely forgot my wife's birthday. My wife thought that was quite remarkable, but I was able to explain it to her.'

General Bedell Smith told the German delegates that the objects of the meeting were:

1. To arrange to feed the Dutch population,

HRH Prince Bernhard, Commander-in-Chief, Netherlands Forces, receives a bouquet of lilacs from the hands of Marietje and Corrie Kok and their mother on the occasion of the birthday of HRH Princess Juliana. On the right hand side of the photograph, the RK-1, Seyss-Inquart's former car can be seen now bearing an Allied star on the trunk.

political prisoners, internees, displaced persons and POW's in German Occupied Holland.

2. To discuss certain proposals for a truce in Holland which had been sent by Seyss-Inquart to the Allied Command.

The American General told the German Reichskommissar that since the occupying power was no longer able to fulfil its responsibilities for feeding the Dutch adequately, he, acting on behalf of General Eisenhower, was authorized to state that the Allies were prepared to assist in this humanitarian duty. General Eisenhower was not prepared to accept too many conditions in this matter and Germans who hindered the execution of this task would be considered to have forfeited their rights to be treated ultimately as prisoners of war. With regard to both the induction of food and the question of a truce Bedell Smith told the Germans of the Allied

ALLIIERTES KOMMANDO
(Supreme Headquarters Expeditionary Force)

MEDEDEELING
aan de Bevolking van bezet Nederland

1. De vijand, die verantwoordelijk is voor Uw voedselvoorziening, heeft verzuimd voldoende voorraden aan te voeren, terwijl de verbindingen met Duitschland nog open waren. Nu hij door onze krijgsverrichtingen geïsoleerd en belegerd is en het misdadige besluit heeft genomen om tot het laatste toe verzet te blijven bieden, zal niet in staat zijn, U voor honger te behoeden.

2. Daar Uw voedselvoorraden uitgeput zijn, heeft de Opperbevelhebber last gegeven, dat onmiddellijk levensmiddelen door vliegtuigen boven bezet Nederland moeten worden afgeworpen.

3. Wij waarschuwen den vijand dat dit zal gebeuren en dat hij onze pogingen om U te helpen niet mag verhinderen en bemoeilijken. Zelfs indien hij mocht probeeren dit te doen, dan zullen wij toch voortgaan alles te doen wat in ons vermogen ligt om Uw leven te redden.

4. Die levensmiddelen zullen door vliegtuigen van allerlei type worden afgeworpen, voornamelijk door zware bommenwerpers. De toestellen zullen laag vliegen en hun last daar afwerpen, waar deze het gemakkelijkst door U kan worden verzameld. Wij kunnen U niet tijdig zeggen waar levensmiddelen zullen worden afgeworpen, en U moet daarom de volgende instructies nauwgezet in acht nemen:

   a. Verwacht voedselpaketten zoowel bij dag als bij nacht. Geeft dus van nu af aan acht op onze vliegtuigen.

   b. Vormt, onder leiding van verantwoordelijke personen, groepen om naar vliegtuigen uit te zien en de paketten te verzamelen. Wij geven den vijand instructies U zooveel mogelijk te helpen. Slaat die hulp niet af: ze zou Uw last kunnen verlichten.

   c. Als gij onze vliegtuigen hoort aankomen, moet gij in plaatsen waar de paketten zonder kunnen vallen, dekking zoeken. De paketten zullen niet met valschermen worden neergelaten en ze zullen zwaar genoeg zijn om, als ze U mochten raken, U ernstig letsel toe te brengen of zelfs te dooden.

   d. Zet, als onze vliegtuigen naderen, op vastgestelde punten wachters uit, om vast te stellen waar de paketten neerkomen.

   e. Verdeelt het voedsel onderling eerlijk.

   f. Als de vijand probeert Uw voedsel te stelen, of als hij probeert om onze vliegtuigen te schieten, noteert dan zorgvuldig alle mogelijke bijzonderheden, en vooral de namen van hen die dit doen. Meldt deze bijzonderheden. De leden van de vijandelijke strijdkrachten, die zich hieraan schuldig maken, zullen als oorlogsmisdadigers worden beschouwd en wij zullen ze als zoodanig behandelen.

5. Let wel — wij kunnen niet beloven in ieder gebied het juiste aandeel van de paketten af te werpen. In sommige deelen zal het aandeel te groot, in andere te klein zijn. Zorgt daarom zelf voor een eerlijke verdeeling.

6. Vergeet niet — wij zijn Uw vrienden en wij zullen voortgaan alles te doen wat in ons vermogen ligt om U te helpen.

BEKANNTMACHUNG
an die deutsche Garnison der Festung Holland

Ihr wisst genau: Vier-einhalb Millionen holländische Zivilpersonen verhungern hinter Euren Linien.

Ihr wisst genau: Die Reichsregierung ist nicht mehr Träger der tatsächlichen Regierungsgewalt. Ihre Autorität beschränkt sich auf einige wenige Widerstandstaschen in Deutschland.

Ihr wisst genau: Das deutsche Heer besteht nicht mehr als geschlossene, einsatzfähige Waffe.

Und doch befolgt Ihr noch immer den verbrecherischen Befehl, bis zum Äussersten Widerstand zu leisten. Euer Widerstand bedeutet für Tausende holländischer Zivilpersonen den Hungertod und für Holland noch grössere Verwüstung.

Um in dieser Endphase der Kämpfe die Leiden der holländischen Bevölkerung zu lindern, hat der Alliierte Oberbefehlshaber angeordnet, dass die holländische Bevölkerung durch Abwurf mit Lebensmitteln versorgt werden soll. Für diese Lebensmittel-Transporte wird eine grosse Anzahl von Flugzeugen aller Muster bei Tag und bei Nacht eingesetzt werden. Diese Flugzeuge dienen nicht den Zwecken des Krieges. Sie dienen der Hilfe für eine notleidende Bevölkerung. Sie werden in niedriger Flughöhe einfliegen und sich aller Aktionen enthalten, die in irgendeiner Weise die militärischen Operationen beeinflussen könnten. Es wird keine Bombenabwürfe geben, keinen Bordwaffenbeschuss und keine Angriffshandlung. Auf Anordnung des Alliierten Oberbefehlshabers ergehen daher an Euch folgende Weisungen:

1. Wer den alliierten Flugzeugen, die Lebensmittel für die holländische Zivilbevölkerung befördern, Abwehr entgegensetzt oder sie an der Durchführung ihrer Hilfsmission zu hindern versucht, begeht ein Verbrechen gegen die Gebote der Menschlichkeit. Wer ein solches Verbrechen begeht, entweder indem er den Befehl gibt, Feuer auf unsere Flugzeuge zu eröffnen, oder indem er einen Befehl dieser Art ausführt, muss gewärtigen, dass er am Tage der Abrechnung für seine Tat zur vollen Verantwortung gezogen wird.

2. Wer den Versuch unternimmt, die von den Alliierten abgeworfenen Lebensmittel der holländischen Bevölkerung zu entziehen, begeht gleichfalls ein Verbrechen gegen die Gebote der Menschlichkeit und wird gleichfalls zur vollen Verantwortung gezogen werden.

3. Es ist Euer eigenes Interesse, bei der Verteilung der Lebensmittel an die holländische Zivilbevölkerung nach besten Kräften mitzuwirken.

---

successes, such as the entry and surrounding of Berlin, the cutting off of Holland and the union of the Allied and Soviet Forces, which made Germany's position hopeless. He advised Seyss-Inquart to cease hostilities and assist in the rehabilitation of Holland as soon as possible. He warned Seyss-Inquart that he was already on the Allied Black List of War Criminals and told the German that sooner or later he would be shot. Seyss-Inquart answered: 'That leaves me cold.' General Bedell Smith's answer was to the effect that this type of execution generally did. Then a private talk between Sir Francis De Guingand and Seyss-Inquart took place. The Germans declared that they would be willing to do anything in their power to provide every possible assistance in feeding the Dutch immediately, provided it did not entail the Allied Forces entering or flying over unmolested areas. These areas, which appeared to be vital to the Germans, were the Hook of Holland and Voorne

Before the actual drops, Allied aircraft dropped leaflets announcing the coming food assistance.

On the other side of the leaflet, the Germans were ordered to abide by the terms of the agreement.

The English artist, Henry Smith, who himself participated in Operation Manna as a crew member of No. 90 Squadron, made this etching called 'Loading the Groceries – 90 Squadron'.

Many pilots were shocked by the view of the watery landscape where once cows grazed and wheat grew.

Island, the IJmuiden Naval Base and the Fortress of Den Helder.

General Bedell Smith mentioned the three major principles on which the experts would draw up their detailed plans. These principles were:

1. Air dropping would take place as soon as practicable on a greatly extended scale. The Dutch distribution facilities could only handle those supplies arriving at no more than 10 dropping zones and they could not safeguard or distribute supplies which arrived by night.

2. Sea supplies would be permitted through certain ports.

3. Inland waterways from the Hollands Diep to

Along the road from Wageningen to the Grebbeberg, the Canadians had piled up large food stocks. The food was transported under a white flag to a neutral zone near Rhenen where it was prepared under German guard for transport to the cities.

On the photograph left, two German military policemen can be seen.

Rotterdam, from Arnhem to Utrecht, and from Kampen to Amsterdam would be used as soon as barges and ships could be provided with waterways swept clean of mines.

The Germans were willing to allow food to come by road, but the Dutch would require assistance from the Allies in the way of motor transport vehicles and fuel to assist in the distribution. The matter of coal to help rail distribution would also be favourably considered by the Allies if it was used solely for feeding the Dutch by rail.

Of course the Germans put forward various stipulations. General Bedell Smith said that they would be dealt with by the various Sub-Committees. The Sub-Committees then went to individual class rooms to discuss their tasks.

Air Commodore Geddes, together with Group Captain Hill and the interpreter, Captain Goodden, sat opposite the German delegates. Geddes made he following notes after the discussions with the Germans:

'Generalleutnant Plocher was accompanied by Major Groebe and Oberleutnant Von Massow. Groebe was responsible for the preparation of the dropping zones. Von Massow was the Intelligence Officer of the 6th Para. Division. He was probably present for German Intelligence purposes. Von Massow spoke English well.'

Air Commodore Geddes stated that the Allied air forces required complete immunity as to the time when the operations were to be carried out and the areas over which the aircraft would fly. Generalleutnant Plocher answered that his orders did not permit such conditions and he insisted on three originally large danger areas near Voorne, IJmuiden and Den Helder. The meeting then came to a deadlock and Air Commodore Geddes referred back to General Bedell Smith for instructions. General De Guingand then came to the meeting to say that the Allies were prepared to accept danger areas being included in the discussions. One problem was the area North of Hilversum. Air Commodore Geddes refused to agree in view of the flooded area of that part of the country and the increased distance the inhabitants of Bussum and Huizen would be forced to travel to collect the food. Major Groebe, who was reponsible for the marking of the dropping zone, agreed to refer back to higher authority and to pass a message

God, oh God! There they come!

'Everywhere we ▷ saw cheering and waving Dutchmen.' (On the photograph, people living in the Laakkwartier of The Hague.) The shadow of a Lancaster skims over a windmill. ▽

via the special wireless link to the Canadian Army to say whether the zone North of Hilversum was acceptable or not.

Finally the two delegations reached an agreement. Air Commodore Geddes wrote it in pencil before the Germans were removed to be taken back to the Canadian lines for their passage to their own troops. It was agreed that the Air Commodore would meet the German delegates again the next day at the village of Nude between the Allied and German forward defended localities west of Wageningen. The time of the meeting was set for 1300 hours. It was not until 1700 hours that the German controlled radio in Hilversum informed the people of the Allied food drops. This German broadcast from 'The Fortress Holland' informed the people that the Germans had accepted the given fact that food was being dropped. In a last attempt to give themselves some importance, the Germans tried to make the people believe that Manna had only

been possible thanks to their own generosity:

'In accordance with the arrangement between the German authorities in the Netherlands and the Allied High Command, Allied aircraft dropped food at points fixed by the CO of the German Armed Forces. British reports say the Allied aircraft had strict orders to adhere to the instructions laid down by the German Command. Other British reports divulge that 200 aircraft dropped a total of 600 tons of foodstuffs. It should be remembered that this is only enough to feed of the population of The Hague for 24 hours. A few days ago the Reichskommissar proclaimed that 1,000 aircraft would be necessary to feed the population of a medium-sized Dutch town for one day. No undue importance must therefore be attached to this sort of Allied relief action. Moreover it cannot be overemphasized that this is a purely Dutch concern and that the German occupying power took part in this arrangement solely in the interests of the Dutch population. People cannot be sufficiently warned against drawing political or even military conclusions from this favour granted by the German occupying power. The military situation is in no way affected by this special action in the

Netherlands. Despite such unusual happenings the war will go on. Every German in the Netherlands and at home knows the war will only end when the danger of alien rule over Europe is banished and the right of every European people to develop its own national life is unconditionally acknowledged.'

Two hours later another German message was broadcast in Fortress Holland. It was additional proof that the situation was changing rapidly.

'As from tomorrow, May 1, the curfew hours during which the population may not appear in the streets will be altered to 2100 to 0400.'

The next day, May 1st Air Commodore Geddes, accompanied by Group Captain Hill and carrying the copies of the agreement in English and German together with two duplicate maps showing the agreed danger zones arrived at a ruined cottage, No. 118 Wageningen Road, Nude, escorted by Captain McAlpine, Liason Officer 1st Canadian Corps and a driver, Private Smith, Canadian RASC, in a Canadian touring car marked with a white flag. The Germans were represented by Oberleutnant Von Massow, a German Luftwaffe Private as interpreter and a large party of German officers and other ranks of the 6th Parachute Division.

Oberleutnant Von Massow said that the German Generalleutnant was inside his own lines and that he would take the necessary documents to him and return them at a stated hour, which was fixed at 1900 hours the same day, signed by responsible delegates. Air Commodore Geddes and Group Captain Hill then signed 4 copies of the German translation, 4 copies of the English translation and the 2 marked maps, which the Germans took with them for signature.

At 1900 hours the same evening, Air Commodore Geddes with the same party and car, arrived at the same cottage and was met by Oberleutnant Von Massow and his interpreter. They handed to Geddes and Hill two English versions of the agreement and one map, all of which had been signed by the German delegates. The German delegates' signatures consisted of those of Dr. Schwebel and Generalleutnant Reichelt, Chief of Staff to General Blaskowitz, Commander of the German 25th Army, Commander in Chief Netherlands and at one time, the Commander of the German Army Group 'H'. The meeting was very quick and both sides

The smoke from the 'Target Indicators' showed the way to the aircraft which followed the Pathfinders. On the photo, Terbregge with the Kralingsche Plas in the background.

*The crew of Lancaster HK 784, JE 'P for Peter'
of No. 195 Squadron; l.-r.: Lee (bomb aimer),
Beavis (flt engineer), Currie (navigator),
Fairlie (rear gunner), Ketley (mid-upper
gunner), and Walters (wireless operator).*

returned at once to their own lines, the German
party leaving in a motorcycle and sidecar.

At about 1922 hours Air Commodore Geddes
telephoned from a Canadian telephone in the
village of Wageningen to 1st Canadian Corps
and as previously arranged passed a message
saying that the agreement had been satisfactori-
ly signed. Thus the operation which had already
started on April 29th could officially begin on
May 2nd...

Air Commodore Geddes and Group Captain
Hill then left by car to the north end of the
Arnhem bridge where they met their own trans-
port to take them by road back to HQ 2TAF.
There A/Cdr. Geddes reported the success of
the mission to Air Vice-Marshal Broom, the

Senior Air Staff Officer at about 2220 hours.
Andrew Geddes had all reasons to be satisfied
with the results of his well-prepared encounter
with his German opponents. For the agreement
see next two pages.

The same day, May 1st, General Foulkes discussed the transport by road and waterways
with General Reichelt. The Germans agreed on
the creation of a corridor, extending south from
the railway linking Arnhem and Utrecht to the
Waal at Ochten. Within these bounds there
would exist a temporary truce, until such times
as the feeding arrangements had been concluded. Foulkes explored the possibility of
extending the area of truce north to the IJsselmeer, but Reichelt was very reluctant. Now food
started pouring in by road, river and air.

In the context of this book, too little attention
will be given to the aid by road and waterways.
But we gratefully acknowledge the tremendous
efforts of the Swedish Merchant Navy.

*The flight path of the Lancasters on 30th April
1945.*

ARRANGEMENTS FOR AIR SUPPLY OF FOOD TO THE DUTCH

1. The following arrangements have been agreed at Achterveld at a meeting at 1800 hours British Double Summer Time/German Summer Time between Allied and German delegates representing General Eisenhower and Reichskommissar Seyss-Inquart. The delegates were:

Allied	German	Dutch
Air Commodore Geddes	Generalleutnant Plocher	H.G. v.d. Roemer
Group Captain Hill	Major Groebe	C.J. v. Schelle
Captain A.C. Goodden (Interpreter)	Oberleutnant Von Massow	

Object
2. The object of this agreement is to start a maximum air supply of food to the Dutch population as soon as possible by means of Allied aircraft.

Safeguards
3. It is agreed that complete immunity south of a line east of Den Helder of the Allies operating over occupied Holland will be given by the Germans in the immunity area marked on the attached signed map. This immunity area includes the sea route from the air bases in England to the dropping zones in Holland.

4. The danger areas in Holland within the immunity area where Germans will not grant immunity in Holland are as follows:
a) BRIELLE danger area: Land enclosed by a line joining TER HEYDE – VLAARDINGEN – HELLEVOETSLUIS.
b) IJMUIDEN danger area: Land enclosed by a line joining ZANDVOORT – HAARLEM – Canal to WESTZAAN – Canal to KROMMENIE – railway to CASTRICUM in a direct line westwards to the sea coast.
c) DEN HELDER danger area: Land enclosed by a line joining DEN HELDER – coastline to HIPPOLYTUSHOEF – east shore of AMSTELMEER – triangular lake at MOLENS – straight line to STOLPEN – south shore of ZWANENWATER thence to the nearest point on the sea coast west of ZWANENWATER.

5. The Allies undertake that during the dropping periods of 0700 hours daily no Allied aircraft will operate in German occupied Holland South of a line drawn East-West through exclusive DEN HELDER danger area except for the sole purpose of dropping food to the Dutch.

6. The Germans on their part undertake to give adequate warning to Allied aircraft which accidentally infringe the danger areas defined above by firing red lights before opening fire when aircraft are within the danger area.

Period of Air Supply
7. The period for air supply will start at 0700 hours British Double Summer Time/German Summer Time on Wednesday May 2 1945 and last until 1500 hours British Double Summer Time/German Summer Time same day. It will continue daily thereafter during the same periods until arrangements are made for it to stop by means of a broadcast announcement of behalf of General Eisenhower from his Headquarters.

Dropping Zones
8. The following dropping zones are agreed:

Serial No.	Plan	Map Reference (English)	Description
51	THE HAGUE	678953	Open space
55	GOUDA	896933	West of Town
57	LEIDEN	730018	Airfield
70	ALKMAAR	938545	Airfield
80	UTRECHT	189924	West edge of Town
81	SCHIPHOL	9816	Airfield
82	VOGELENZANG	849182	Open space
83	YPENBURG	685875	Airfield instead of Waalhaven
84	KRALINGSCHE PLAS	790755	

The following site will be confirmed by the Germans by wireless to the Canadian special set in Holland:

74	HILVERSUM	243090	Bussumer Grintweg

Method of delivery
9. The method of delivery will be that of free dropping of packages. Target indicators may be used, dropped from aircraft, to mark the dropping zones.

...king of the dropping zones

The dropping zones will be marked with a
...e cross to mark the centre. Green lights fired
... the ground will indicate that the aircraft are
...pping correctly. Red lights fired into the air
... indicate that aircraft are entering a danger
...a.

...esday 1st May, 1945   HOLLAND

...gnature of delegates for General Eisenhower
...d Reichskommissar Seyss-Inquart.

...ritish	German	Dutch
...J.W. Geddes	Schwebel	no signatures
...ir Cdre	Reichsrichter	
...H. Hill	Reichelt	
...G/Capt.	Generalleutnant	

Overview of the major supply lines.
Operation Manna – food supply by the RAF
Operation Chowhound – food supply by the USAAF
Operation Faust – food supply by the Canadian Army
Further food was supplied via the major rivers, through
the Nieuwe Waterweg and across the Zuiderzee.

Dropping zones:

1	Waalhaven	7	Valkenburg
2	Terbregge	8	Hilversum
3	Gouda	9	Schiphol
4	Ypenburg	10	Vogelenzang
5	Duindigt	11	Bergen
6	Utrecht		

*After having dropped the food, the Lan-
casters bank away from Terbregge.*

Fetching and transporting

For two Dutch people Manna had a very special meaning. One was a Wassenaar woman, the other an Amsterdam-born Flight Lieutenant who was the captain of a No. 90 Squadron Lancaster.

LEVENSMIDDELEN

● Deze levensmiddelen zijn voor U. Zij worden U gebracht door Geallieerde vliegers en zijn uitsluitend bestemd voor Nederlandsche burgers. Zoekt dit heele gebied af voor het geval er paketten buiten het vastgestelde gebied zijn gevallen en voegt bij Uw voorraad. Gebruikt de levensmiddelen niet voordat Uw verantwoordelijke leiders ze verdeeld hebben en gij Uw rechtmatig deel hebt ontvangen. Als de vijand probeert er zich meester van te maken, noteert dan alle bijzonderheden meldt deze. Blijft naar ons uitzien. Wij komen terug.

● Diese Lebensmittel sind ausschliesslich für die holländische Zivilbevölkerung bestimmt. Sie sind nicht bestimmt für die deutsche Wehrmacht oder das Wehrmachtsgefolge. Jeder Angehörige der deutschen Wehrmacht oder des Wehrmachtgefolges, der diese Lebensmittel entwendet, trägt dadurch zur Hungersnot in Holland bei und macht sich eines Kriegsverbrechens schuldig, für das ihn die gerechte Strafe treffen wird. Steht der holländischen Bevölkerung nach Kräften bei!

LEBENSMITTEL

Between December 1944 and March 1945, Yvonne Boichel had made four long hunger tours covering a distance of almost 1,000 miles. The first tour began during the week before Christmas and took her six days. Yvonne walked and cycled from The Hague to Leiden, Utrecht, Amersfoort, Zwolle, Heerenveen and finally to Langweer in Friesland and back. The total distance she covered was no less than about 300 miles.

During the second week of January 1945 Yvonne, this time accompanied by a friend, again left for a long voyage to find food. This time the two young women travelled almost 350 miles. From The Hague they went to Leiden, Zeist, Amersfoort and Apeldoorn. Having had little luck there, they headed north to Meppel and Leeuwarden. Ten days later they returned

On 29 April one of the food parcels fell in the garden of the house of the parents of Yvonne Boichel on the Pr. Frederiklaan in Wassenaar. With the parcel was a white carnation. The label, warning the Germans not to steal the food, is still in her possession.

home. Again they had succeeded in buying some food.

As the end of the war came closer, the food situation grew worse. During the first week of February Yvonne Boichel and her friend went to Deventer. Six days later they came home. More than 180 miles had been covered. Then the last week of February came. Again Yvonne said goodbye to her parents and joined the stream of people roaming the countryside hoping to find some food somewhere. Yvonne Boichel remembers: 'This time I went alone. I took a pair of wintershoes with me to exchange for food. As the Germans from February 10th had forbidden the people in Western Holland to be in the streets after 1700 hours I had to be careful when I came back. After having spent the first night in Zeist I arrived in Apeldoorn the next day. Nobody was willing to sell me some rye or other foodstuffs if I had no goods in exchange.

My money had literally lost its value. Only things like shoes were accepted. At the house of my host I had to wait for a long time. He had other people who wanted meat and perhaps there would be something left for me. No need to tell that illegal slaughtering was very heavily punished if found out. Downstairs I heard loud voices and discussions going on about who was to get what. At last the door opened and I was handed a paper bag. I received some cracklings, that was all. Of course I was grateful but on the other hand I felt terribly disappointed having to return home with almost nothing. As the Resistance had warned the people that the Allied fighters would shoot up any vehicle visible on the roads, travelling home was a bit risky. We had to be extremely careful. At some moments I had to take cover in a porch and wait until all was clear again. The fighters operated alone or in pairs.

Finally I reached our house. The tears came running down my eyes because of the failure to find food. Mother said that I should bring the cracklings to our neighbours. They were six people, all grown-ups and as thin as bean stalks . . .

At the end of April we heard rumours about the food drops. On April 29th it finally happened. We heard the sound of roaring engines. The sound came closer and closer. Then we saw the aircraft. We waved like mad, we danced and jumped. One of the most precious memories I have was the sight of a single parcel tumbling down. It fell straight into our garden. I rushed to it and carried it into the house. We were crying with happiness. Then we saw something printed on the top lit. It said in Dutch and German that the food was to be distributed among the Dutch and that it had to be taken to a collecting centre if dropped outside the area. I decided to cut off the text and keep it forever. Then I rode to the Duindigt horse race track and handed them the parcel. Five days after the drops we received the first Allied foodstuffs. What a change it was. No sugar beets or tulip bulbs. Biscuits, chocolate, meat, all dainties we had not tasted for such a long time.'

When the war broke out Hans Heukensfeldt Jansen was a Cambridge student. The young Dutchman was very shocked when his country was overrun. At first he volunteered for the Land Army. However he felt that picking peas was not really a contribution to the liberation of his fellow countrymen. He decided to volunteer for the Royal Air force.

On May 26th, 1941 'Heuke' Jansen made his first familiarization flight in a Tiger Moth. On October 16th, while still in training, he survived a crash landing. That day his instructor F/O Rose took him for some night flight training. While trying an overshoot the Miles Master suddenly lost power. The engine cut. Immediately Rose tried an emergency landing. He managed to land his plan in the trees. There the aircraft caught fire. Heukensfeldt Jansen, himself wounded, managed with great difficulty to

F/L Heukensfeldt Jansen (in the back row in the middle of his air crew) flew as a skipper with No. 90 Squadron. The ground crew is kneeling in front. His log book read 'Lancaster R – Food dropping, Rotterdam, 2:55 hours.'

save his instructor from the burning wreckage. A few days later, Heukensfeldt Jansen left the hospital.

On February 28th the Dutch Ministry of Defence in London accepted him as a reserve-second lieutenant/pilot. Some time later he received his commission as a Pilot Officer in the RAF. About two weeks later he was awarded the British Empire Medal for the courageous rescue of his instructor. In April 1942 he swore an oath as an officer in the presence of the Captain of the (Dutch) General Staff, H.J. Kruls, who would become a sort of viceroy of the Netherlands immediately after the liberation, during the

period when the Netherlands remained under the rule of the Military Authority.

Now P/O Heukensfeldt Jansen had to follow the long road of training in all sorts of aircraft. In August 1944 he flew Wellingtons.

After being promoted to reserve-first lieutenant/pilot, 'Heuke' Jansen became the captain of a heavy bomber. By March 1945 Flight Lieutenant Hans Heukensfeldt Jansen was flying with No. 90 Squadron. His aircraft, called 'Cherokee', took him on various missions. On March 22nd, he attacked Bocholt, on March 27th, Altenbogge. On April 9th he took part in the raid against Kiel and wrote in his logbook 'Admiral Scheer sunk!!' During the month of April, Heuke Jansen 'paid visits' to Kiel (13th), Potsdam (14th), Heligoland (18th) and Regensburg (20th). On April 25th and 27th he was ordered to fly an apparently odd exercise: dropping sand bags, followed by a low level navigation exercise. When the food drops were commemorated in the Netherlands in 1970, Heukensfeldt Jansen wrote down how he felt when he was told that he was to fly Operation Manna: 'We got orders to fly practice drops first. We had to find a small field at our base and drop little sand bags. On April 30th my crew and I got up early and went to our bomber to watch the loading of the Lancaster. The sacks were put on the bomb doors. As the bomb bay was filled the doors were further closed. When no more sack

△

Lancasters of No. 635 Squadron (PFF) marked Ypenburg Air Field on 3 May 1945.

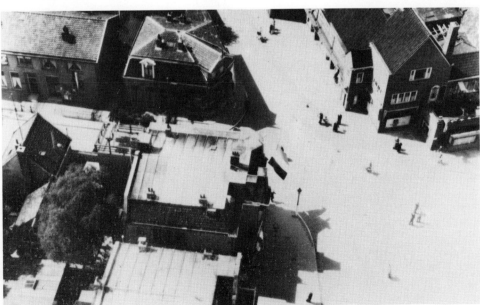

▷

'During the briefings, we were told to fly very low . . .'

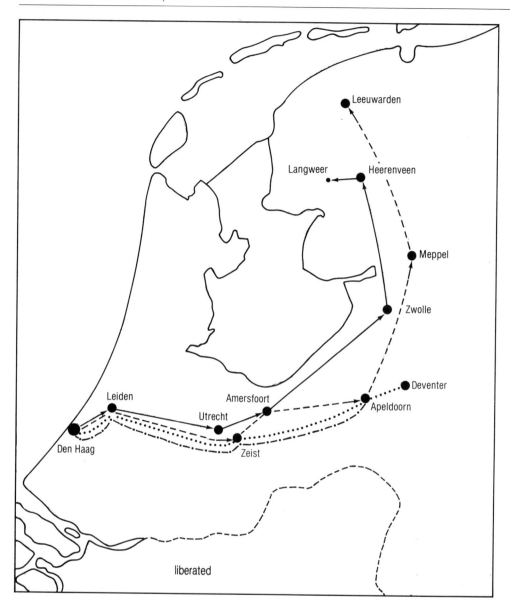

De famine tours of Yvonne Boichel.

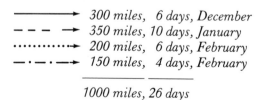

——————→	*300 miles, 6 days, December*
– – – →	*350 miles, 10 days, January*
·············→	*200 miles, 6 days, February*
–·—·—→	*150 miles, 4 days, February*

1000 miles, 26 days

could be stacked through the narrow gap the doors were completely locked. Unfortunately a few sacks got stuck between the doors. Therefore they had to open the doors again. This was done a little bit carelessly and suddenly the entire load fell on the tarmac. During the briefing we were told to fly very low.

Soon after take-off we reached the Dutch coast. The inundated areas were clearly visible and looked very desolate. It made a deep impression on us. The water had entered the houses. But

Waalhaven Airfield on 30th April seen through the rear turret of a Lancaster. In the distance, another Lancaster approaches Rotterdam.

still we got the most marvelous welcome from these houses. Everywhere flags could be seen to celebrate the birthday of Princess Juliana. Everywhere people were seen waving at us. These things made this particular April 30th unforgettable for us.

When we approached Rotterdam and came closer to the drop zone I had to force myself to concentrate on the approaching course. A quiet voice could be heard saying: "Left, left, keep her steady, right, right, keep her going like that skipper, Pathfinder markers straight ahead, right on top of it, Skipper." It was the voice of Charlie (McIntosh) our Canadian Bomb aimer. For me it was an unforgetable memory. I always considered it a privilege that I being a Dutchman had been allowed to deliver this precious cargo to the brave city of Rotterdam.'

At the beginning of the drops the Dutch authorities had to work under great pressure. German help could not be expected. It would in fact be very pleasant if the Germans refrained from hinderance. From Dutch documents recently found in the hands of a private individual we now know a little more about the problems that had to be faced by the reception committees. We traced documents about the organization of the drops in the Rotterdam area, written by the responsible authorities. The events here will not be much different from the situation at the drop zones of Ypenburg, Duindigt, Valkenburg, Vogelenzang, Bergen, Schiphol, Hilversum, Utrecht and Gouda.

The men responsible deserve our full admiration for what they managed to achieve and for the responsibility they dared take when faced with suddenly setting up an entirely new organization. One of them was W.Th. ten Bosch, responsible for food supplies in the Greater Rot-

terdam area. On Saturday 21st April Mr. W.Th. ten Bosch received information through Resistance channels that within a few days Allied aircraft would drop food. Three days later this information was confirmed by the BBC. Ten Bosch believed it to be necessary to contact the German authorities. After having tried in vain during the early afternoon, Ten Bosch was finally admitted at 1600 hours. Völcker's reaction was very blunt, 'Rubbish'. Besides, the plenipotentiary had not heard anything from the Wehrmacht. However that same afternoon when another meeting was in progress at the Rotterdam townhall, Völcker said that indeed an Allied supply plan was under consideration. However the Reichskommissar had turned down the proposed plan and had ordered his anti-aircraft batteries to fire upon Allied aircraft trying to enter 'German' airspace. German announcements appeared everywhere in Rotterdam saying that the Allied plans had been turned down.

That evening at 2300 hours, Ten Bosch, Verbeek and Van Wijk were summoned to appear at Völcker's office. There they met the Nazi burgomaster of Rotterdam, Müller, and the German official responsible for food problems Chur. Müller told the three men that the food drops would be carried out after all. Ten Bosch and his aides were asked to do anything possible to help the food drops to be a success. They were to start their work immediately . . .

One of the assigned drop zones was to be the aerodrome of Waalhaven, abandoned and rendered unserviceable by the Germans. In September 1945 Mr. Ten Bosch wrote in his report:

> '[it was] decided to place a number of carts and groups of volunteer labourers at this zone. We expected enforcements lat-

'And the people called it Manna . . .'

er that day. During the night the shifts of Oranjeboom Breweries would be sent to help us.'

Flares fall from a Pathfinder Lancaster at Terbregge.

Thursday April 26th, a few moments before the collecting teams were to be sent out a courier of the German plenipotentiary arrived.

Waalhaven was not to be used as a drop zone. In its place another zone near Terbregge, northeast of Rotterdam was chosen. Waalhaven had not been completely cleared of mines and it was situated too close to the docks.

Immediately the working party was sent to Terbregge. Later that morning Völcker's arrived, accompanied by Burgomaster Müller, Alderman Duikhuis, Völcker's secretary Mayer, the inevitable functionary for food matters Chur and the German police liason officer Fellmayer. Also present were Messrs. Ten Bosch, Verbeek and Van Wijk. The German Green Field Police as well as the ss had also sent their representatives to Terbregge.

An area beside the municipality of Hillegersberg had been chosen as the drop zone. At the east, it was bounded by the Terbregseweg, on the north by the quay of the Rotte River and on the south by two roads called Ceintuurbaan and Spiegelnisserweg. The zone was in a very bad area, the Alexanderpolder, over 20 feet below sea level. In order to drain it a separate pumping engine had to be used. Besides that the terrain itself was most unfavourable. Every 50 yards the grassland was divided by deep ditches. The heavy rainfall of the last couple of days had soaked the area. As there was no electricity, the pumping engine no longer functioned. The emergency pumping engine was also not yet working. This caused the water to stand at ground level. Various parts of the drop zone had been completely flooded. Another problem was

The crew of Lancaster AR 'L for Love' of No. 460 (RAF) Squadron ready to take off for Rotterdam on 3rd May 1945. Standing l.-r.: H.G. Johnson (pilot), Chris Smith (bomb aimer, wearing an apron for the occasion), Jack Salmon (flt engineer), Bill Rail (navigator), Alan Ritchie (wireless operator). Kneeling l.-r.: F. Fleetwood (mid-upper gunner) and R. Prance (rear gunner).

the fact that the terrain was practically inaccessible for horse drawn carts. It would have been possible to use carts with rubber tires, but since no such tires were available, all packets would have to be carried away to the roads by hand. Immediately, the planning committee understood that great difficulties would occur during the collecting and transportation of the food. They protested to the Germans but the latter would not change their minds. The area had been picked by the Wehrmacht: no further discussions. The committee could however do nothing else than accept. The Technical Service of the town of Rotterdam however thought they would be able to improve the situation. They managed wonderfully by laying over 2,000 yards of steel plates in the fields thus creating provisory roads.

In spite of all these difficulties and the lack of cooperation from the Germans, the 'Rotterdam Manna Committee' worked with great energy. Within two days an organization was created to receive and transport the food in an orderly way. Two 'terrain commanders' were appointed. They both received an assistant. The terrain commanders were responsible for the entire drop zone. Their assistants were made responsible for the reception of the food.

Mr. Derksen, one of the authorities, asked the Crisis Controle Service, an organization founded to prevent black marketeering, to supervise the drop zone. The Rotterdam Municipal Police was to guard the perimeter and to prevent theft. Rotterdam's industry supplied the committee with the hand and means of transportation. The first men came from the Heineken and Oranjeboom Breweries.

When the drops started the German attitude

Flying at an extremely low level, a Lancaster roars over the Dutch landscape.

was harsh. The Germans controlled the roads with the Rotterdam Police. Völcker however issued an order that no one would have access to the drop zone unless they had a German permit. Soon there were many complaints. The police complained that the Germans used Wehrmacht vehicles and had denied the police the right to check these. The Germans accused the Rotterdam police of theft. After consulting the President of the Rotterdam Court and the Public Prosecutor, Völcker decided to withdraw the German troops. Court officials were sent to check the police. Now the police complained about the officials being thieves. There were many problems between the police and the customs officers. In short, one institution was obstructing the other.

Initially the Luftwaffe was made responsible for the drop zone, as in their eyes they were the only ones capable of dealing with air matters. The Luftwaffe received warnings of approaching aircraft by telephone from Amsterdam and The Hague. The Luftwaffe would then inform the

Until 5 May, German soldiers guarded the food dropped at Terbregge.

SD, the German Security Police. The SD was to warn the Dutch. Soon however, the hated SD disappeared, followed by the Luftwaffe on 6th May. After that day the Dutch Interior Forces took over the protection of the drop zone. On Saturday April 28th – the first British drop had been postponed due to the bad weather – another meeting was held in the Rotterdam Exchange. During the meeting the final lines of sight were drawn. Mr. M. Pool, representative of the highest Dutch authorities in The Hague, was present at this meeting. One of the conclusions was the designation of the factories of Jamin and Sillevoet as storage centres.

The next morning many people gathered at Terbregge, looking out to see the RAF coming. The RAF indeed came, but apparently they had not been informed of the change of drop zone. The Lancasters dropped their cargo at Waalhaven aerodrome . . . There was of course no one present there to collect the food. The entire reception team was quickly sent to the aero-drome again. Fortunately Mr. Van Wijk had witnessed this drop and sent people to the airfield. Local farmers volunteered to salvage the food. Unfortunately a lot was dropped into the Waalhaven dock. In addition quite a few individuals had been able to steal food. Another part had to remain on the airfield as it had fallen in the middle of a mine field. By around 1600 hours the next day the food had been removed from Waalhaven and stored in the 'Maas' flour mill. Soon another problem arose: the help given by civilians. The three men responsible believed that the work had to been done on voluntary

This Lancaster of No. 153 Squadron flew 46 operational missions before the crew brought food to our country. From l.-r.: Jock Whitting-stall (flt engineer), Peter Speed (pilot), Robby Bates (navigator), Colin Hill (wireless opera-tor), Alan Fowler (mid-upper gunner), Cyril Meadows (bomb aimer) and Jack Mitchell (rear gunner).

basis. The volunteers came in great numbers, sometimes expecting to obtain something for themselves, but mostly only with the intention of helping. Soon it became clear that these people were weak and underfed. Therefore they could not achieve much. All of them were standing in the mud, dragging and carrying the heavy sacks over too long of distance.

Theft was punished severely. In order to prevent robbery, food was distributed during the drop itself when no one could enter the zone. But in spite of this strict surveillance, theft could not be completely prevented. Sometimes people tried to eat from damaged tins and sacks. Even organized attempts to steal cart loads were made; the police caught the robbers red-handed. Thanks to the CCD, the 2nd. Section of the Rotterdam Interior Forces and the Municipal Police, these attempts all failed.

Approximately 5-10% of the food dropped came down in ditches and canals as well as in the nearby lakes. Here too the major part of the food could be salvaged. Damaged parcels were sent to the hospitals, the Interclerical Aid Fund and other assisting institutions.

Fortunately there were for the most part few accidents, although some people were hit when a few Lancasters dropped food over the Kralinger Hout Park. Minor accidents happened when people cut their hand on broken tins. Nevertheless, the village of Terbregge suffered heavy damage. Five houses burned down after Pathfinder markers hit the roofs. Some sheds burned down as well. This damage was reported in the Operations Record Book of one of the Pathfin-

Two views of the Kralingsche Plas. Above: in 1945 with two overflying Lancasters. Below: the same neighbourhood in 1984.

ders Squadrons. Many tiles were damaged when sacks of food crashed on them. This caused 'some nervousness' among the Terbregge villagers.

Soon it appeared preferable to use barges for the transport of the food. After the food had been collected and brought in on carts and wagons, it was taken to the Rotte-quay where the barges were waiting. Approximately 265,000 parcels and sacks were taken to Rotterdam this way. Again the men and women did a fine job. Responsibility for the 'shipping' fell to two gentlemen, Messrs. Binkhorst and Wepster. Marvelous work was done under command of this duo. Thousands of volunteers carried the food from the drop zone. The carriers were told to which barge they should take their load. This ensured a smooth delivery. Two tugs pulled the barges to the final storage locations, the Paul C. Kaiser factory and the Van Nelle factory. A total of 91 shiploads were transported by 55 different barges.

It was necessary to regularly provide the workers with food. At first they received the chocolate bars that were among the dropped foodstuffs. Later individual meals were cooked at the quay. The carriers got their food by showing a special coupon.

One incident should be mentioned here: One of the CCD-officials was hit by an English sack of food while he chased someone who had tried to steal food. The official suffered a double fracture of the leg. The report did not mention whether the thief got away.

From 1st May, American Flying Fortresses joined the Lancasters. Here a B-17 of 390th Bomb Group drops army rations over Valkenburg Air Field.

A Santa Claus in May

After the final agreement with the German authorities had been composed on April 30, General Foulkes discussed with his opponent, General Reichelt, the desirability of enlarging the area of truce from the IJsselmeer coast to the banks of the Rhine. Reichelt would not agree. The Allies decided not to wait any longer and started the operation.

On Monday April 30th the drops were flown without any appreciable difficulties. The Germans had practically withdrawn from the drop zones and left all further work to the Dutch. That Monday about 975 tons of food came down in the agreed fields. However Waalhaven, being heavily mined by the Germans and being too close to the docks, turned out to be unfit for its purpose. Instead of this zone, a piece of land northeast of the Kralingsche Plas, a large square lake, was chosen.

From Tuesday May 1st the number of drop zones was increased. The Americans, using B-17G Flying Fortresses, visited the British zones the first day and dropped 776 tons while the Lancasters of the RAF dropped no less than 1,046 tons. The USAAF dropped 10-in-1 or 'K'-rations, the combat food normally issued to the American soldiers.

Apart from Americans and Britons, many other

Anglo-Australian crew of a No. 460 Squadron Lancaster. L.-r.: Sgt O'Conners (wireless operator), Sgt Leaviss (RAF, rear gunner), Sgt McCluskey (RAF, mid-upper gunner), Sgt Barrie (navigator), Sgt Collins (RAF, flt engineer), Sgt Munro (bomb aimer). Kneeling, Flt/Sgt Lewis (pilot).

nationalities took part: Canadians, New Zea-landers, Australians, Poles and even some Dutchmen who were in RAF squadrons.

For the crews of the Australian No. 460 Squadron this kind of 'warfare' was an exceptional experience. On May 1st the Air Ministry issued a special news bulletin for the people in far away Australia:

'An Australian Lancaster squadron of RAF Bomber Command flew with many other squadrons to drop food in Holland yesterday, Monday morning. Some of the Australian crews were making their first flight over the Continent and others were nearing the end of their operational tours. One of the latter, Flight Lieutenant K.W. Finlay, a pilot, from South Perth, spoke of the accuracy of the dropping in spite of trying weather conditions.

He said the Dutch gave the Lancasters an enthusiastic welcome. Flying Officer B.S. Mulcahy of Melbourne, a pilot, who has made 28 bombing trips said there were three guides to the target. They were able to identify the aiming point visually and also by target indicators and a white cross.

Another pilot said: "The Dutch were standing out there in the rain, waving anything they could get hold of. Some had Union Jacks and were standing right by German soldiers. It gave me a great thrill to see their obvious excitement as we skimmed the roof tops. This is better than bombing every day."

Flight Sergeant J. Howard, a rear gun-ner from Sydney, told how some of the crews had decided to make the Dutch a personal gift. They saved up their bars of chocolate and made their own para-chutes. "As we dropped our bundle," he said, "we suddenly realized that other people had had the same idea, and little parachutes full of chocolate were falling like snow-flakes, wherever we looked. We chose a pleasant little back garden to deposit ours and saw a Dutch woman dash up to the bundle as it fell on her lawn. Howard was of the opinion that this had been the best way to show how the aircrews felt about the Dutch."'

Later that day Radio Resurgent Netherlands broadcast a special report which came in Dutch and English after the news:

First speaker: 'Ladies and gentlemen: When on Sunday night I heard the eye-witness account of the dropping of food supplies by the RAF, when I heard how the people of The Hague crowded the streets and greeted the aircraft, I grew cold with emotion and did not know how we could thank God and those who made this possible. One who has never really known hunger cannot imagine what this means, nor can he realize the feelings of gratitude which rose in the hearts of the people of Rotterdam, The Hague, Utrecht, Leiden, Delft and other inhabitants of starved cities when the Allied promise was fulfilled. You, the inhabitants of the German occupied countries, will not have been able to suppress your tears. What you felt that very moment cannot be put into words. Having come myself only recently from occupied Holland, the great privilege falls to me to-night of expressing your feelings in front of this microphone – to convey most fervently the heartful thanks of the starved people of Holland to you, General Eisenhower, to you King George of England, to you Winston Churchill, to you gallant men of RAF and to you in England who have pleaded for our starved countrymen. In name of occupied Holland, I thank you all and most sincerely hope that the day will soon come when those who received your precious gifts will be able to express their gratitude themselves.'

After this a second Dutchman spoke; this time on behalf of the already liberated part of the country:

'That part of Holland which is now free of the Germans has more than once conveyed its thanks to all Allies and friends. But the joy of freedom was spoiled by worry about the fate of our countrymen who still live under the yoke of German tyranny. That worry for so many of our family and friends, for so many of our countrymen in the West, has now been lessened. The liberated part of Holland, in relief and new hope, addresses itself to all who brought this happy change.

Our thoughts go out to the Allied Supreme Command who organized this work of salvation. We think of all air crews who, as we have learned, enthusiastically fulfilled this human task. We think of all who collected this life saving food, who packed and transported it and to those who in any way assisted in executing this urgent work.

We thank all, of all ranks, whoever they are, wherever they may be, we are very grateful to them indeed. It may mean relief from the greatest need and we hope that the future will bring the blessings that come with all acts of humanity, to all those who have done their share.'

After the agreement between the Allies and Germans had been realized, a great mass of food poured into the still occupied part of Holland. Along roads and across the sea enormous stocks were produced. The overland operation, called 'Faust' was executed by the Royal Canadian Service Corps, assisted by the Royal Service Corps of the British Army. All these units were under command of a Canadian officer with a very Dutch name, Lieutenant-Colonel DeGeer. Up until 10th May 1945, the Canadians and Britons managed to get approximately 1,000 tons of food per day into the Occupied Territory, totalling no less than about 8,500 tons. On May 1st the USAAF joined in, flying the silver Boeing B-17G Flying Fortresses from various airfields in East Anglia. The combined efforts of the Allies Forces saved the Dutch, especially the people living in the cities around the dropping areas.

Operation Faust. From Wageningen Canadian and British trucks drive to a neutral area near Rhenen where Dutch drivers will take the wheel and drive into occupied territory.

It was my best flight pay

The enthusiasm of the men who participated in Operation Manna is reflected in the official despatches of their squadrons. In the records of the 156th Squadron, for example, the following is stated: '30.4.45. The squadron carried out its first food supplies mission over Rotterdam. The starving people greeted the airplanes with cheers.' On May 1, 1945, the War Diary of the 15th Squadron stated: 'The Hague. Food dropping mission. Twenty one airplanes were allocated to drop supplies over The Hague. All airplanes took off and found the target, which was marked with a white cross and flares. Many people in the target zone were waving flags, including some Union Jacks. Even some Germans waved. A Red Cross car was seen near the target. Kraut patrols on the coast. Weather bad with spells of rain.' Another entry: '7th May 1945. The Hague. Food dropping mission. Twenty six airplanes were allocated to drop food supplies. The weather was clear. We could not fly very low. Some of the ration bags burst because they were dropped from too great a height. Many people were waving flags. "Thank you boys" was written on one of the roofs. We also saw requests for tobacco.'

Had the crews expected these reactions? What did they know of the Netherlands and its situation? William F. Jones, Intelligence Officer at RAF Hemswell, was aware that the food situation in the Netherlands was deteriorating and that the Dutch population was in a desperate situation. 'Almost all the food supplies had been commandeered by the Germans and the Dutch population was at the brink of starvation. They had told us there were no Dutch children younger than twelve months and only a few younger than three years old. For the past nine months, almost no babies had been born to the undernourished mothers. To relieve this situation [. . .], Bomber Command was given permission to drop food supplies from a low altitude. No shots would be fired at the aircraft. However, we had to adhere to specifically assigned flight routes, times and other instructions.'

The flight crew had mixed reactions to the food dropping missions. Flight Lieutenant Sarsfield-

Squadron Leader Bill Jones was the Intelligence Officer at RAF Hemswell. In his book, Bomber Intelligence, *he gives a vivid description of the food drops he took part in.*

Inset right page:
Flight Sergeant McAllister and his crew in Lancaster JB-613, IQ-Y for Yorkie.

THANK YOU
BOYS

Kelly, a pilot, remembered there was scepticism, especially during the initial briefings, about the agreements made with the Germans. 'There was some speculation that the Germans would wait until most of the aircraft was flying above their territory so they would have easy prey to shoot at.' Another pilot, Flying Officer Richard Barrister listened with dismay to what was expected from himself and his crew during the coming days. 'Haven't we gone through enough already? Which idiot organized this? How in God's name can they believe that the Germans won't fire at us? As soon as we've dropped the rations, they'll shoot us down and confiscate the food. Why run the risk of losing dozens of crews. Are the Dutch really in such desperate distress as we've been led to believe. The country is so fertile.' There were different opinions also. 'I remember that some crew members were angry and disappointed when they heard they had not been selected for Manna. Especially those who had seen such terrible things and felt responsible for the damage their bombing raids had caused, wanted to help in some constructive way,' said Warrant Officer Jim Davis, a Lancaster rear gunner. Still others had a change of heart. Frank

Wedge, for example, a member of the 115th Squadron's IL-H for Harry Lancaster crew, said, 'The flooded lands, the destruction of Rotterdam, the visible poverty all changed our minds about Manna. I remember that some fairly crude remarks were made when we heard during our briefing on April 29 that we would fly in low over the Netherlands with German permission. It was a strange sight: the German gunners followed us with the barrels of their guns and we had our machine guns pointed at them. I think they would have won if their promises had not been kept . . .' This fear was shared by others. Bomb aimer Flight Sergeant Gibson was also worried. 'Our first flight plan into Holland gave us extremely low altitude. While I concentrated on the dropping zone, the pilots concentrated on flying and we all tried not to think of the danger of enemy fire below.'

Practice flights, using sandbags, were made before the actual rations could be dropped. According to Sarsfield-Kelly, 'the run-through was executed at an altitude of 150 metres with the landing gear down, flaps one quarter down and flying at minimum speed. It became clear during these practice flights that these were the

P/o Diack (pilot) and Flt/Sgt Paterson (flt engineer) heading for Duindigt in their 12 Squadron Lancaster.

▷

After a successful drop at Valkenburg, a Lancaster flies over Rijnsburg and turns west, back to England.

Thousands of volunteers helped collect the food, as can be seen at Duindigt.

only conditions under which a sandbag could land undamaged. Anything more or less would cause the bag to burst open.' Gibson said, 'No one had any idea how long it would take to drop the entire load of food. We couldn't estimate the speed of a falling bag of powdered eggs. As the bombaimer, I just set my sights on the lowest possible level and hoped for the best.' Another problem was the loading of the planes. Roy Moore, who was assigned to RAF Elsham during the last months of the war, remembers clearly how difficult it was to load the Lancasters full of rations. 'We packed all sorts of food into the Lancaster's bomb bay and that was really difficult. We had to close the doors first and then open them just enough so that a man could climb in. The ration bags were passed to him one by one and stowed in the bay. It was hard to keep the bags from falling out again, but this was the best way of stowing the largest number of rations. The payload was two or three tons. It took two to three hours to fill the plane. We

worked long days – 16 hours a day was not unusual. Loading food supplies also turned out to be more difficult and time-consuming than loading bombs. When the plane taxied out onto the runway for a normal bombing run, usual practice was to test the bomb doors. The bomb aimer would open the bays once or twice. However, one of the take-offs for a food mission went wrong because of this practice. We sweated over two hours to load our Lancaster full of supplies for Holland. We said our good-byes, started up the engines and taxied out to take our place in line. Suddenly we noticed to our dismay that the bomb doors had opened and the rations were all over the runway. The base commander jumped in his car and drove after the plane. The crew were ordered to repack the payload. This did not improve their temper.'

Sarsfield-Kelly made his first ration dropping over Rotterdam on May 1, 1945. He was given careful instructions: 'We were ordered to fly a specifically assigned route from south to north at an altitude of 150 metres with flaps at 45° and our speed at a minimum. One minute intervals were to separate us. After we had made our drop, we had to make a 90° turn to port and return home. If the drop had been unsuccessful, we had to turn 90° to starboard and rejoin the planes on their way to the dropping zone. This was the sort of briefing we were given before flying to The Hague on May 2, 3, and 7. The dropping zone was south-east of the city. All my runs were successful, and each time I turned 90° to port so that I often flew right over the city. The flights were very short; I think about 140 and 180 minutes long.'

Although the flights were usually of short duration, they were also very interesting. William

Jones and the crew of Lancaster TC *'P for Peter'. On 5th May, he accompanied Australian Flt Sgt Richardson and his crew to Rotterdam.*

Duindigt race track photographed on 1st March 1945. Left, the large anti-tank ditch which surrounded The Hague. On the right, the Landscheidingsweg.

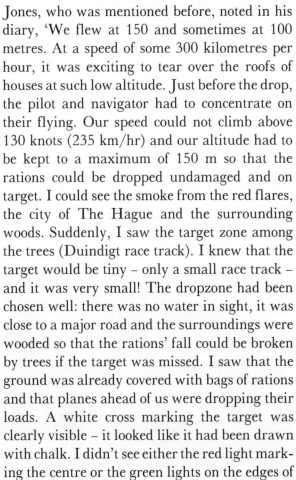

Jones, who was mentioned before, noted in his diary, 'We flew at 150 and sometimes at 100 metres. At a speed of some 300 kilometres per hour, it was exciting to tear over the roofs of houses at such low altitude. Just before the drop, the pilot and navigator had to concentrate on their flying. Our speed could not climb above 130 knots (235 km/hr) and our altitude had to be kept to a maximum of 150 m so that the rations could be dropped undamaged and on target. I could see the smoke from the red flares, the city of The Hague and the surrounding woods. Suddenly, I saw the target zone among the trees (Duindigt race track). I knew that the target would be tiny – only a small race track – and it was very small! The dropzone had been chosen well: there was no water in sight, it was close to a major road and the surroundings were wooded so that the rations' fall could be broken by trees if the target was missed. I saw that the ground was already covered with bags of rations and that planes ahead of us were dropping their loads. A white cross marking the target was clearly visible – it looked like it had been drawn with chalk. I didn't see either the red light marking the centre or the green lights on the edges of

Ypenburg after the drops.

Coming from Rotterdam, this Lancaster heads for Ypenburg. Below, we can see the Delftsche Schie Canal and in the distance, the city of Delft.

the target. However, these were really unnecessary because the red flares on the west side of the track were so bright. I saw a Dutchman waving enthusiastically close to the target marker, unaware of his danger. At 16:56 the bomb aimer dropped the payload and the pilot opened up the throttles, increasing our airspeed as ordered. Both the rear gunner and the bomb aimer reported that the load landed exactly on target and that a few of the bags ended up just outside the zone in the woods. The race course was covered with bags of food.' Jones' diary gives a good idea of how the dropping zones were located. 'We were given 4 targets for Operation Manna, which were all in the area of The Hague and Rotterdam: Valkenburg airbase near Leiden, Ypenburg near Delft, the race track just north-east of The Hague and an area on the north shore of a large lake called Noordplac (actual name Kralingsche Plas) north-east of Rotterdam. These targets were small and we had to read our maps carefully in order to follow the correct route. In addition to the white crosses with the red lights in their centre, the Pathfinder Force was supposed to drop red markers above the targets to assist the flight crews.

Ypenburg airfield was the target for our first Manna mission. The drop was scheduled for 13:45 and all our planes were in the air by 12:09 after the planes were loaded.

Some of the crewmen were worried about having to fly so low over an area that was still in German hands. In the end, however, everything went well and there were no serious incidents although a few of the aircraft were hit by German fire. We dropped about 90 tons of rations. The next day, April 30, 39 aircraft were sent out on a second 'Spam' operation. I attended the briefing and flew the mission in L for Love of the 150th Squadron under command of Flight Lieutenant Callington. A total of 91 aircraft had orders to drop their payloads above a target formed by the ellipse of a race track in the woods north-east of The Hague. Zero hour above the target was 12:30 p.m. The route was a simple one flying from Southwold to the island of Overflakkee, over some islands in the river delta, between Vlaardingen and Maassluis keeping Rotterdam to starboard. Here began the actual approach, which went over Delft. Ypenburg airport was a good landmark. The Hague lay to port. After the briefing, I went to the aircraft to prepare the crew. We still had two hours before departure so we had some time to relax. However, before we could run through our check list, zero hour was postponed to 16:45 and English air space had to be cleared by 17:15 instead of 16:53. Before departure, we therefore had time to eat dinner, which we really appreciated. After finishing, we went back to our planes and got ready to leave. There were no further delays and at 14:53 we taxied out to the runway, taking off

at 14:54. We had 40 minutes before we had to be on our course so we made our usual crosscountry flight to Glossop over the Pennines with a beautiful view of the hills and lakes before flying towards Hemswell. Then we set our course for the Dutch coast. As usual, the weather was not good with low clouds at about 500 m. Above England there was fog, with rain and hail. We had to fly through heavy rain and decrease our altitude to get out of the cloud cover. It was raining over the sea as well, but there was enough break in the clouds to see that better weather was ahead. At 16:43 we passed over the Dutch coast near Overflakkee. To starboard, I could see the Flying Fortress that had been reported by the crews on the last run (probably B-17G, 43-9297 of 490BG which had crashed on the beach near Ouddorp after an emergency landing on April 5, 1945). In the distance, I also saw the lighthouse on the western tip of the island. I began to recognize some landmarks. A

'Below I saw people running to collect the food . . .'

With bomb doors open, 2 Lancasters fly to Terbregge.

lot of land was flooded and in some places we could just see the tops of windmills, houses and farms above the water. It looked peaceful enough, but we realized that much had been destroyed below us. When we turned towards the last stage of the route, we flew into a rain storm which badly reduced visibility. It only lasted a short time though and the weather improved again. We saw more farmland, but everywhere were signs of flood. When we approached the drop zone, we saw a field of yellow tulips. Then The Hague appeared in front of us.'

Apparently the Netherlands made such a strong impression upon the low flying airmen, that many still remember it 40 years later. G.R.V. Haynes, a Lancaster commander, still clearly envisions the groups of people waiting to pick up the ration bags on the ground. 'We were worried that they would be hit by the falling bags. It was a strange sight to see the German tanks with their guns pointed at us near the dropping zone when we arrived on the first day. We were flying so low that we could see the faces of the Germans sitting in their tanks.' Wing Commander R.A. Jell was a pilot, commanding 218th squadron in 1945 at raf Chedburg, a few kilometres west of Bury St. Edmonds in Suffolk and he has his own memories of the 'grocery flights'. 'I flew to Rotterdam and The Hague. The things that I saw will always remain in my memory – especially the extensive flooding of your country. The image of an old man who was driving a horse and cart along a dike with only water on either side of him as far as the eye could see; the few roofs pointing out of the water was a depressing sight. It was a nicer experience to see the people out on the roofs of houses waving orange flags enthusiastically. Some had written messages on the roofs like "Thanks RAF" and "cigarettes please". Along the roads and near the race track, William Jones saw Dutch people with wheel barrows, bags, and carts of all sorts ready to go out onto the dropping zone and gather up the rations. We gained altitude above The Hague and set our course for the coast and home. Flying over the city, I saw still more people waving and cheering. It looked so peaceful that it was difficult to imagine that the Dutch were still under German occupation. It was even more difficult to realize that the German anti-aircraft gunners had set their guns to shoot us down at the first wrong move we made. At the coast, I could even see one of the German guns turning in pursuit of us.

How we would have liked to attack those German troops and gun positions, but we had issued strict orders to all crews to hold fire which also meant we could not change course or descend to observe the situation below more clearly. If those guns had fired at us, they would have greatly damaged those planes flying at low altitude which were very vulnerable. Any evasive action at that low height would have been useless, especially because there were so many aircraft. We passed over the Dutch coast while taking a last look at the celebrations in The Hague.'

Jack Western was a rear gunner in a brand new Lancaster. His plane didn't have a name yet and the crew had not had a chance yet to paint a logo on the craft's nose. 'We understood that the war with Germany was almost over', remembered Jack. 'One day, we were told that we would be dropping food to the starving Dutch instead of

'Spamy': the dwarf carrying a bomb in his back pocket and a tin of Spam in his hands.

One of the Lancasters was so new that the Manna Operations gave it its name, Spamy. The crew of this No. 153 Squadron bomber were l.-r.: F/o Martin (pilot), Sgt Western (rear gunner), Flt/Sgt Gray (mid-upper gunner), Sgt Baker (flt engineer). Sitting l.-r.: Flt/Sgt Fenerty (bomb aimer), F/o Eisen (navigator), and W/o Enstran (wireless operator). The young man on the far right is a ground crew member of whom we only know his nickname, 'Peewee'.

◁ *In the cockpit, navigator Joe Eisen.*

bombs. We thought this was grand and put our heads together. I made a design for the nose painting and decided on a name. One of the crew members drew a dwarf wearing a pair of over-alls with a disarmed bomb in the back pocket and holding a can of Spam in his hand. Spam was universally known in those days and good bargaining material if you could get hold of it. It was a sort of luncheon meat and tasted like something between ham and corned beef. We called the plane "Spamy" and I'll never forget how we flew into the Netherlands at an altitude of 60 m. On the way home, we went all out. The pilot, a Canadian, flew at sea level. When we passed over Western Holland on our way home, we flew by a windmill and people waved at us from its balcony. You understand, we had to look up to wave back!'

Looking out from his position in the rear gun turret, Sergeant Kenneth 'Timber' Wood saw his Lancaster flying towards some particularly high chimneys. 'Two men were sitting on them waving down at us. I waved back. Never seen anything like it in my life. Because I was sitting at the rear of the plane, I had more time to notice things. People were everywhere – on the streets, on the roofs, leaning out of the windows. They all had something to wave with; a handkerchief, a sheet – it was incredible!' These experiences made an indelible impression upon the crews. Flight Sergeant Gibson said, 'I will always remember seeing "Thank you Tommy" written on one of the roofs and one old lady leaning out of an attic window to wave at us. While the food was being parachuted down into the dropping zone, I saw people waving and running to the sacks, picking them up despite the danger of being hit by our Manna. I couldn't say if we were thankful at the time, but I know that each mission was an emotional experience. I will always remember those flights as a beautiful experience, it was as if we brought the liberation closer to reality.'

More was dropped than just the official ration bags. During each flight, the crews were issued their own rations – candy, chocolate and the like. 'Because we didn't really need them ourselves', said Sarsfield-Kelly, 'we made parachutes of our handkerchiefs and dropped our rations over the city with a note that they were to be given to the children.' Jones had another method: 'On May 7 I brought along 100 cigarettes accompanied by a message in Dutch and the Sunday papers. I jettisoned the cigarettes from the rear turret over what I took to be a main street of Rotterdam. The newspapers I dropped on the grounds of a hospital on the north side of the harbour. The other aircraft also dropped newspapers, cigar-ettes and chocolate bars fastened on to para-chutes made of handkerchiefs.'

Wood had stowed his gunner's turret so full of supplies that he could barely move. 'Once we were above Holland, the bomb aimer and pilot signalled me that I could start dropping my own rations so I jettisoned packages of powdered eggs and tea from our Lancaster.'

Bomb aimer Joseph Gildea called the Manna flights 'NAAFI runs'. On May 1 he wrote in his diary: 'Another NAAFI run today. One hundred ninety Lancasters delivered food. The Dutch people waved at us from roofs and street corners. After we dropped our cargo, we flew over the city at roof height. I used the Aldislamp to signal "V for Victory" from the forward turret and that made the people even more enthusiastic.' For-mer First Lieutenant Chris Malcolm also had his own memories of Manna. 'It seemed as though the people below us were unconcerned about their own safety. They ran like mad onto the field where the ration bags were falling like stones. We had stowed extra bags into our Lan-caster GI-E for Edward, PD 366 and told the bomb aimer he should drop them near an iso-lated house. While the dropping was taking place, the bomb aimer was yelling his comments through the intercom. He went wild when our

Forty years later, l.-r.: Ken Wood, Chris Malcolm and Norman Walters.

'Malcom's Madcaps'. Sitting on the port inner engine of their No. 622 Squadron Lancaster. L.-r.: w/o Ricky Windon (wireless operator), Sgt Bill Webster (flt engineer), F/o Chris Malcom (pilot), Flt/Sgt Reg Robinson (bomb aimer), Sgt Norman 'Ginger' Walters (mid-upper gunner), Flt/Sgt Len 'Leafy' Lane (navigator) and Sgt Ken 'Timber' Wood (rear gunner).

extra bags landed behind the very houses we aimed for. "They've got them, they've bloody got them!", he yelled. I had to tell him to shut up because he was making it impossible for the others to communicate with one another.'

Intelligence Officer William Jones remembered his emotion at the time. 'I think we all had tears in our eyes upon seeing these people waving and cheering, knowing that they had suffered so much under the German occupation. Many were carrying Dutch or British flags which must have been hidden for a long time. Everywhere we saw the simple way in which they expressed their gratitude for what we were doing. It gave us a feeling of single-minded purpose; those ration bags would be dropped right on target.'

On Liberation Day Jones flew over Holland. 'In the streets I saw people distributing tulips and selling flags laid out on wheel barrows. It was evident that this Liberation Day meant a great deal to the Dutch, who had been waiting for this day so long. A large building in a major street was full of waving and cheering people. I saw a tulip field in which the words "Tabac" and "Thanks RAF" had been cut out of the red and yellow flowers.'

This was not the only way in which the Dutch

expressed their gratitude. A few weeks after the German capitulation, a letter was delivered to RAF Witchford, Frank Wedge's home base. The envelope was simply addressed 'To the pilot of IL-H, RAF, England'. It was a thank-you letter from a Dutchman who had seen the aircraft from his fourth-floor bedroom window after it had dropped rations not far from his home.

What was the reaction of the Germans to all this? One bomber was seen to leave its column and drift out of the flight path assigned by the Germans. A flare was immediately launched from the ground to order the pilot back into line. This was within the context of the agreement between the Allies and the Germans, but didn't make the pilot's minds rest easier. Gildea noted in his diary, 'We could see the Germans manning an anti-aircraft gun which was following us in its sights. I could feel my heart thumping.' Gildea's fears were not without reason. Jell's airplane was hit by hand gun bullets despite the agreement which had been made.

Others had similar experiences. Steward Menaul, commander of the Pathfinder base at Upwood, flew 'H' Lancaster of the 156th Squadron on April 30. 'We had to mark the dropping zone near Rotterdam. It was a fairly simple exercise, we were flying at low altitude, assuming that the Germans would keep to their agreement and leave our planes alone. Anyway, if they had fired at us we had no chance to return fire. We were also carrying some food, which we dropped at the same time as our markers. After the drop had been completed, our rear gunner reported that some Germans positioned on a dike had shot at us. Evidently they wanted to let off some of their frustration. Even though our own guns were loaded, we did not return fire.'

Powerless rage. That must explain the reaction of the 'tall German standing on top of a sand dune shaking his fist at us as we flew low over the Dutch coast'. Flying Officer 'Monty' Monteith gave him a fitting response – he made a 'V

Group Captain Steward Menaul was one of the Pathfinder pilots. At the end of the war, he was O/C RAF Faldingworth.

for Victory' sign with his fingers!

It must be said, however, that some flyers were perhaps overly enthusiastic. On May 3, Gildea noted that there was a large grandstand full of German soldiers at the dropping zone (Duindigt race track). 'I decided to give them a good fright. I waited until my bomb sight indicated one degree off the grandstand. At that point, I dropped our payload. The Krauts must have seen that the rations were dropped too late. Good heavens, what a panic broke out! They climbed over each other to get out of the way. The ration bags dropped right in front of the grandstand. It was a beautiful sight!' Jones saw something similar happen from his aircraft. 'A Lancaster was flying right in front of us with its bomb bay doors still open. One of the ration bags had probably jammed them, because when the plane approached a battery of artillery, I saw a

bag fall and land on a gun surrounded by German soldiers. The bag burst open and covered them with flour, while they were scattering in all directions.' On May 5, the crew of Jones' airplane decided to do something special. 'I was watching a group of Germans marching along a river bank. Suddenly, the plane dropped her nose and we dived towards the shocked Germans. No hesitation at all, most of them jumped into the river . . .'

'Timber' Wood still feels he owes an apology to some Dutch people. 'During the flight, I kept throwing packages out of the turret. At one point, we were over an area with many greenhouses and my packages went through their roofs like cannon shots. I hope that their contents was reasonable compensation for the damage.'

'Monty' Monteith experienced a more serious situation. 'The dropping zone – a large field north-east of Rotterdam – had to be marked in the shape of a cross with "Drem lights". A Lancaster Pathfinder had also dropped red target markers as an additional aid. One of these flares fell about 750 metres past the target and onto the roof of a farm bordering the drop zone. The house immediately caught fire. I felt so sorry for that poor farmer whose house had withstood the terrible attack on his city in 1940 and which was subsequently destroyed by the Royal Air Force on a mission of mercy.'

The flying crews remember Operation Manna with gratitude, as do the Dutch. Sarsfield-Kelly has been back to Holland many times since the war. 'I have met Dutch people who have expressed their admiration and gratitude once

◁ *Duindigt: police-men collect sacks and boxes on 1st May 1945. The food was brought hence to The Hague via the Waaldorperlaan by horsedrawn wagons.*

they heard I was a member of the RAF and helped supply them with food. It makes me feel that Operation Manna was useful, after all those terrible things that happened.'

Gildea's last flight was on May 7. 'Those Manna flights had a special meaning for me. As a young scout, I had participated in the 1937 World Jamboree at Vogelenzang. The hospitality of the Dutch people then made a deep impression upon me and in 1945 I was given the change to do something in return.'

Monteith: 'Thinking back on my visit to the Netherlands in 1983, I feel especially proud to have been able to play some small part in an historical event like Operation Manna; an occurrence which is so engraved in the hearts of the Dutch.'

Wood remembers, 'That first food dropping was the most emotional and impressive event in my entire life. I am still proud of the small share I had in Manna.' When Jim Davis' children ask him 'what was the most important thing you did

The crew of Lancaster PD-364 dropped food at Terbregge on 30th April and at Ypenburg on 1st and 3rd May 1945. In the squadron they were known as Charlie Ainsworth and his Bremen Busters. Standing l.-r.: Flt/Sgt Phil Irving (rear gunner), Flt/Sgt Ron Burrows (navigator), Flt/Sgt Chas Ainsworth (pilot), Flt/Sgt Trevor Priestly (bomb aimer), and Flt/Sgt John Smith (flt/engineer). Kneeling l.-r.: Flt/Sgt Bruce Wymer (wireless operator), Flt/Sgt Peter Lawrence (mid-upper gunner).

in the war, daddy?', he invariably answers, 'the Manna missions I flew over Holland. It suddenly made everything we did seem of value.'

Thanks Yanks!

For the American 95th Bomb Group, the month of May also carried a pleasant surprise. Rather than spreading death and destruction, they were allowed to drop life-giving food. During six 'Chowhound' missions, more than 500 tons of food were dropped.

Enthusiastic crowds near the dropping zones showed their gratitude by waving flags. Somewhere in occupied territory, an unknown person cut out the words 'many thanks' in a tulip field. The crews participated in the missions with relish. The flights were also interesting to them because they were carried out at low altitude. Literally, the flyers had a front row seat.

The group also suffered losses. The B-17G 44-8640 was returning from a supplies mission above the Netherlands. Halfway across the North Sea, the inner port engine burst into flames. The pilot feared a mid-air explosion and ordered the crew to bail out. Staff Sergeant David Condon remembers how he sat in the bombardier's seat checking the compass when the navigator touched his shoulder and pointed out the window. 'I saw nothing unusual and turned back. Suddenly I noticed that the plane was full of smoke. A few minutes later the navigator disappeared through the escape hatch forward. He managed to open the door against the pressure of the wind and jumped out. In the meantime, the photographer, who was sitting with me in the nose, and I strapped on our parachutes. The photographer jumped out via the forward escape hatch. I tried to take a one-man raft out with me but couldn't. I couldn't wait much longer because at the same moment, I saw a ball of fire drop past me. I think it was either the engine or a part of it. I saw that the plane's bomb bay doors were open, Immediately upon leaving the plane I pulled my chute open. Some seconds later I landed with a smack in the water and went under. When I surfaced, I inflated my life vest but didn't unfasten my parachute harness because I thought I would be more visible that way. After a time, however, I became entangled in the lines and had to get rid

Three Flying Fortresses in formation over Vogelenzang.

of the chute. A bottle of dye was attached to my life vest so I emptied its contents into the sead. A short time later I was spotted by the crew of a Lancaster.' After the crew had escaped from the burning plane – it was flying at an altitude of 200 m – the bomber crashed into the grey sea. We can find out more about the tragic aftermath of this crash from the report of the British 550th Squadron which was stationed at RAF North Killingholme.

'At 18:00, thirty aircraft and crew under command of Wing Commander McWaters took off for a Manna mission. The Lancaster returned to England after a successful drop. [...] Flying Officer Handley of BQ-K^2 saw an American plane had come down in the North Sea and was almost submerged. The pilot immediately switched his IFF to "emergency" (Identification Friend or Foe – a transmitter/receiver with which Allied planes could identify one another to themselves and to their air defence systems). When it descended to 60 m, the K^2's crew spotted an American-type rescue raft with a possible occupant. After circling, the crew saw the raft was floating upside down and that it was empty. A ship was seen steaming south about 10 miles from the wreckage. The Lancaster flew towards it, circled the ship and signalled "SOS Follow me". The ship's crew answered from the bridge, turned and followed K^2 to where the B-17 lay half-submerged in the water. In the meantime, the Lancaster's wireless operator had transmitted its position, altitude, etc and had received instructions to remain in the area. When the first ship to be alerted arrived at the scene of the wreckage, her crew launched a rescue boat to search for survivors. About 4 km from the site, the K^2 crew spotted someone floating in the water, still surrounded by a parachute. There was no sign of a life jacket so the tail gunner threw one down into the sea, near the flyer who was able to pull it on. A flare was also dropped to mark the spot. American Flying Fortresses had arrived in the meantime so that the sky was full of airplanes. Two more survivors were spotted east of the wreckage. More lifejackets and flares were thrown into the sea. Sometime later, a Catalina amphibian plane landed on the surface and took aboard the first survivor. A Walrus amphibian also arrived and picked up a second man. While the Lancaster continued to circle, her crew spotted an empty life raft, and launched yet another flare and more life jackets. Almost immediately a third survivor was seen in the water. The K^2's crew alerted the Catalina by radio and dropped flares to guide it to the spot, where the amphibian plane soon arrived to pick up the flyer. After a thorough search of the area, no more survivors were found and the Lancaster returned home to base.'

Only three of the B-'s crew of thirteen were found alive. One died on the way home to England. A short time later, a fourth crew member was found in the water, dead for some time.

Survivor David Condon remembers: 'The bomber circled above me and shot off flares. Some time later a PBY-Catalina landed near me and took me aboard. I had been in the North Sea for about half an hour. In the Catalina I fainted from cold and shock. I only heard later that Lieutenant Schwarz and I were the only survivors. The saddest part was that two members of the crew were flying with us at their own special request. Because the Germans had capitulated, there seemed to be no risk involved, so they had received permission to come with us. Their first flight was their last.'

David C. Condon was one of the two men who survived on 1st May 1945 when their B-17G crashed into the North Sea.

The crews returned home with many stories about flying at low altitude over the Netherlands. According to 'Father Mac', James McCarthy, chaplain to the 403rd Bomb Group,

Briefing at one of the American Bomber Groups on 1st May 1945.

it seemed as though the people of Rotterdam had lost all control of their joy. 'We saw thousands of Dutch men, women and children on the fields, in the streets and on the roofs, waving flags of all shapes and colours. The Fortresses were flying so low over enemy territory that we could see the upturned faces of the German troops. They were looking on passively as the four-engined "Angels of Mercy" brought their loads of deliverance to save thousands of innocent people. I remember that we were flying so low that we could see the wooden shoes worn by the children!' David A. Mullen was the first pilot of a B-17, Third Scouting Force. He flew weather reconnaissance missions. 'We had to precede the bombers to each target in order to inform the 8th Air Force Headquarters and those bombers following us what the local weather conditions were. I remember one dropping zone where cows were grazing, and the farmer came along to chase them out of the way while we circled. That day, cloud cover was between 150 and 180 metres but we never flew higher than 30metres, and had a grand time! At one point during the low altitude flight we saw German soldiers sitting in foxholes. When we flew over that point once more, we saw a German officer stand up and follow us with his binoculars. Then another officer stood up. When we flew past once more, he threw something at us. My navigator became nervous because he thought the Kraut was throwing hand grenades. On the return flight, we followed a road that went over a dike. There, we saw a man riding a bicycle towards us. We descended to tree level to say hello. When he saw us, he jumped off his bicycle and into the canal. Strangely enough, not once did we see our bombers dropping food supplies because we were always flying in front of them. The only exception was an unfortunate B-17 that dropped its load into a canal.'

In 1945, Frank W. Rone was piloting the large B-17 of 388th Bomb Group's 562 Squadron, based at Knettishall. On 1 May, he wrote in his log book that his flight had lasted three hours and fifteen minutes and that he had flown at an altitude of 150 metres. 'The Flying Fortress (or, "Sitting Duck", as we called the plane during this particular flight) does not normally fly at this altitude. We had dropped our load of rations and descended about 100 metres. We continued our flight at about 50-60 metres to have a better view of the people waving below us. We had ten passengers on board, ground service personnel who had their first chance to see something of the European mainland. Suddenly, a tower came into view in front of us that was at least 25 metres above our flying level. My speed of 165 miles an hour did not give me much time. I pushed all four throttles forward at once, pulled the stick towards me and missed the tower by inches. I remember the dead white faces of the passengers. None of them offered me a drink after the flight . . .'

The Americans were just as surprised as the

6th May 1945. A B-17 over Alkmaar.

British when they heard what was expected of them. Compared with 23 missions he had flown above occupied Europe, 19 year old Technical Sergeant Bill Richards felt Operation Chowhound was a whole different ballgame. Richards was a radio operator and machine gunner in a B-17G attached to 863rd Squadron of the 493rd Bomb Group. He had helped bomb almost every important target in Germany and encountered much resistance. Sometimes he asked himself how long his luck would hold out and whether he would return to Debach, his group's home base. He remembered his dismay upon being told what he and his squadron were expected to do. 'They informed us that a cease-fire had been negotiated with the Germans and that we would not be fired upon while we ferried food to the starving Dutch. We were therefore ordered to fly rations to the Netherlands and to drop them over a certain target. The Germans would know our route, our arrival time and pretty well everything else. That was pretty scary and we didn't trust this at all.'

Ralph K. Bragg, crew member of a Flying Fortress attached to 100th Bomb Group, was surprised and suspicious when he heard which alti-

Sometimes the bombers flew so low that they returned to base with branches and cables wrapped around wings and tail wheels. Here, a low-flying B-17 over the Schermerpolder.

tude was assigned to his group. 'In addition, we were used to flying in a formation of bombers in order to protect ourselves as much as possible from attacking fighters. Now we were being ordered to fly one by one to the Netherlands. The officer briefing us said that an agreement had been made with the Germans giving us safe passage if we kept within an assigned flight corridor. We flew to the Netherlands and saw water everywhere. Over the target we dropped our load of bags and boxes. The supplies were not dropped by parachute, as was the case when we dropped weapons, food and medicine to Polish freedom fighters at Warsaw during the uprising. We could not go back and try again if the dropping failed because we would have had to leave the flight corridor and I know the Germans would have shot us down like flies. It was a strange experience to be flying so low over enemy territory. It was also frightening. We saw German anti-aircraft guns surrounded by their crews who were looking up at us. The barrels of their guns followed us along our flight path. I heard later that some of our aircraft were fired upon.'

Despite their fears of a German attack, the American flyers were willing to help out the Dutch, as may be seen fron the story told by 21 year old Lead Bombardier Douglas S. Eden. He had a great deal of luck compared to others of his age. During an attack on Hamburg on New

Years Day, 1944, he was the only member of his crew to survive, because he had stayed home sick that day. Douglas Eden was also a member of the 100th Bomber Group, which was nicknamed 'the Bloody Hundred'. According to rumour, the heavy losses suffered by this group were due to the fact that they had not 'played according to the rules'. After a b-17 of the 100th Bomb Group had been hit by fire from a German fighter, the pilot lowered the bomber's wheels as a sign of surrender. The German pilot, thinking that his opponent had capitulated, flew closer to the bomber, intending to escort it to the nearest air base. At this point, the bomber's gunners were said to have opened fire

Just as the British, the Americans flew a number of test drops, such as this one which took place at Horham Airfield on 25th April 1945.

B-17G, 44-8452 of 493rd Bomb Group, on its way to Vogelenzang.

◁ *Douglas Eden flew as a bombardier with 100th Bomb Group. He considers his last food bombardment at Schiphol Airport as his best: he dropped his load on top of German aircraft.*

at the German fighter. The German was killed and his comrades were supposed to have sworn that all bombers carrying the tail insignia of a 'D' framed by a black square would pay heavily for this death. The truth of this story has never been proven. For Eden, the Chowhound flights were a welcome change from the many missions he had flown under more harrowing circumstances. 'The food flights over the Netherlands were very different. We had been told that the Dutch were starving and that we would be given the chance to save some lives. We were allowed to volunteer for these missions and they would not count as operational flights. We found that this chance of saving lives was worth the risk. After all, these were rescue flights and not flights of destruction! We were ordered to fly as low as possible over the Netherlands – but not lower than 30 metres – and then to climb to about 120 metres after dropping the rations. White crosses would serve as targets. We were also told that a cease-fire had been called so that we could not shoot at the Germans and neither could they shoot at us.'

In order to carry as much food as possible, the planes were made lighter and only four of the usual ten crew members were given permission to go along on the mission – the machine gunners staying behind. Aboard were the pilot, the co-pilot, the navigator and the radio operator. According to Technical Sergeant Richards, 'I felt terribly vulnerable without our gunners. I kept a diary of sorts and when we flew to Rotterdam on 1st May I wrote, "For a bomber, we flew very low, about 120 metres high. On the way out, we flew over Rotterdam and we could see the people leaning out of their windows to wave at us. We also saw Krauts marching in the streets pretending not to see or hear us. After dropping our load, the pilot descended and 'buzzed the ground', which we enjoyed very much, because usually we flew at about 7,500 metres or higher. Some pilots flew much too low, because after a few days we received orders not to imitate fighter tactics. There were stories that some Flying Fortresses had returned with trees, cables and other souvenirs hanging from their wings. Our captain said we were supposed to be helping the Dutch to rebuild their country, not tear it down. Apparently there were even official complaints made about pilots flying so low they had scared people into jumping in canals. But in general it was a marvelous experience to bring people food instead of death and destruction.

While American bombers drop food over Schiphol Airport, the German crew of an anti-aircraft gun have their picture taken. Note the great difference in ages and the various uniforms. On 1st May, the Americans dropped ration boxes at Terbregge. Guarded by Rotterdam policemen and supervised by a specially established committee, the food saved thousands of Rotterdam people from certain death.

Seven times I flew to Holland – Rotterdam on 1st May, north of The Hague on 2nd May. All other droppings were made above Schiphol airport." ' The bomb bays had to be adapted to carry rations. Two wooden panels were attached to one another. The outside of the panel was hinged to the bomb rack while the other side was secured by a cable. The loop at the end of this cable was attached to the bomb-release mechanism. The idea of all this was that the panels would fall open allowing the rations to fall when the bombardier pressed the activator switch. Despite this careful design, the droppings were not always successful. On his first Chowhound mission, Second Lieutenant Reese Martin of 96th Bomb Group went to Bergen. The bombers flew in fairly large formation at the extremely low height of 100-125 metres and low speed. All this made the B-17 a very difficult aircraft to fly, according to Martin. He remembers, 'she kicked like a mule'. 'The second day I flew "Five Grand", a famous airplane because it was the 5000th B-17 built by Boeing. I made a special note of this in my logbook, because flying

in this particular aircraft was considered worthy of note. Her in-and-outside walls were covered with the signatures of the people who had built her. It was a funny thing to see this flying page from a notebook among the other Flying Fortresses. On May 5, our British cousins had taken care of the load, rations stowed in cotton and linen bags. When we approached Schiphol airport, near Amsterdam, I gave the signal to drop our load, but there was no confirmation. I sent my flight engineer, Technical Sergeant Tom Harrison back to see what the matter was. Finally we got a green light that the load had been jettisoned. I looked up and suddenly saw a ghost in white with the features of Tom Harrison. What had happened? A bag of flour had been jammed in the port bomb bay so that the left vent couldn't be opened. Tom had taken his knife and slashed the bag open, letting out the flour. The turbulence caused the flour to fall all over him. The rest of the crew thought it was quite a joke, but Tom didn't see the humour of the situation.'

Ray Powell of the 100th Bomb Group found a different solution when ration bags became stuck. 'On 3rd May I made my first flight. We were told that we would have an escort of P-51 fighters on our port side and German BF-109 fighters would accompany us to starboard. I have never seen a German, let alone a Mustang . . . The dropping zone was marked by an enormous white cross. As ordered, we dropped

Reese Martin (standing left) was the captain of B-17G 'Five Grand'. This aircraft of 338th Squadron of 96th Bomb Group was the 5000th Flying Fortress built. When it left the factory, the people of Boeing covered it with their signatures.

B-17's over Bergen Airfield.
On the right, Bergen Airfield, made unservice-
able. The bombing apparently was not very
accurate.

our load above the assigned target, an airfield near Alkmaar. A few bags remained behind in the storage bay. We couldn't turn back again because of the danger of being shot at by Germans. A few minutes after leaving the target area, I saw an isolated house near the sea. Further along were more houses whose inhabitants had come out to wave at us. We threw the rest of our load out by hand. Later, we took along our own home made packages that we dropped out of the rear turret of the pilots' windows near isolated houses along our route.'

The story told by Engineering Officer Bill Carleton shows that matters can go wrong for other reasons as well. 'I must admit that we made a serious mistake during one flight. During the approach, the bombardier fell asleep and missed the target zone. When the pilot yelled at him over the intercom to wake up, he was startled, pushed the activator button and dropped the whole precious load hundreds of metres away from the dike into the Zuiderzee. I won't repeat what the poor fellow was said to during the flight home or what awaited him upon his return to the base . . .'

Even if the mission went perfect, strange things could happen. Bob Seney was a mechanic and a member of ground personnel. He once went along on a food mission as a passenger. 'I will always remember one thing. We flew right at a large building in The Hague. Cheering people on the roof were waving at us. However, the closer we got, the less people waved. Suddenly they all turned around and started running

B-17 'Goin' My Way' of 95th Bomb Group was the most elegant aircraft during the food drops. The B-17 flew to Holland, provided with white tires. The crew was composed of (standing l.-r.:) Kettler, Kerkwood, Rodriquez, Hayes, Stanley. Sitting l.-r.: Saucier, Harold 'Pappy' Dulle, Thomas and Lykken.

away. They were evidently afraid we would fly right into the building. We roared with laughter. I hope those poor people have forgiven us.' We can be grateful to Harold 'Pappy' Dulle, pilot of the B-17 'Going my Way' assigned to the 95th Bomb Group for this story: 'On May 1, we dropped food over a stadium. Everything went perfect. Then the intercom burst into life with the voice of one of the crew, "Lieutenant, you missed the chimney to starboard by one and a half metres and the ballgunner wants to know what to do about the mud on his windshield'."
Of the various events during the missions, Lead

Bombardier Eden remembers how his plane flew at very low altitude, climbed quickly upon approaching a dike to descend again until it came upon an isolated house or a lonely fisherman. 'I still remember how we climbed to save a fisherman from being buffeted by the wash from the propellers and how he was pushed against a wall by the force of the air. While we descended further, he shook his fist at us . . . I also remember something that looked like a prison camp. The main building had a large red cross painted on its roof. We saw countless arms and hands stuck through the windows waving at us. Dur-

Among the American air crews who participated in Chowhound were a number of men of Dutch descent. One of them was Lt Remmenga, flying with 452nd Bomb Group. Standing l.-r.: Birk (radio operator/gunner), Houghtaling (gunner), Verrilli (ball gunner), Vrechek (tailgunner). Kneeling l.-r.: Remmenga (pilot), Molner (co-pilot), Clabots Jr. (navigator), Maynard (bombardier), and Roberts (flt engineer). They dropped food over Duindigt on 1st May and over Schiphol on 2nd, 3rd, 5th and 6th May.

ing one of my four flights, it struck me that cows and horses would run in fright through fences and gates as we flew over. This was particularly remarkable because it was something unusual for us. When we took off and landed in England, we also flew over pastures and meadows but the animals paid no attention to our noise. It must have been quite a sight from the ground to see a flotilla of bombers approaching and flying over.

Two other things moved me deeply. Seeing the words "Thanks Yanks" written down somewhere or cut out of some vegetation. I was also touched by the fear of two children. I was seated in the plexiglass nose of the aircraft navigating for the entire group. Suddenly I saw two children stop their playing and look up in fear. They ran to a tree and tried to hide. I waved at them but they gave no response. We had come as friends, but how could they realize this?' The Americans have retained good memories of Operation Chowhound. Intelligence Officer Harold Rosenn said, 'we entered the Netherlands at a height of about 150 metres. Above the target zone we dropped the load of K Rations. The weather was fairly good that day and I was touched when I saw letters on the ground spelling out the words "Many Thanks". Approaching a city, we saw people everywhere, both young and old, waving like mad. It was one of the most emotional moments during the two years I served in the war and I have always considered myself privileged to have had such an experience.' Or, as Bombardier Harold E. Province put it, 'We enjoyed these flights and hoped that our work helped the Dutch people.'

B-17G 'Stork Club' flew 5 food missions. On 1st May, it went to Terbregge, on 2nd May to Hilversum and on 3rd, 5th and 6th May to Schiphol.

standing l.-r.: Unkn...
Sitting l.-r.: Hydecke...

On 2nd May 1945 a lone B-17 accidentally dropped food near the Vami Dairy in Purmerend.

members of 'Stork Club' were, stein, DuShane, and Wells. , McCafferty, and Swana.

After the drop over Hilversum on 2nd May, 'Stork Club' was hit by German AA-fire. Pilot Swana, kneeling next to the hole in the wing, had great doubt about the identity of his co-pilot.

It was a miracle . . .

The fear of tomorrow, the worry about what to put on the table the next day were two essential questions to be answered by the people in the still occupied part of the Netherlands. These thoughts do come back from time to time in the minds of the people who survived the days of famine. One of them was J. Vrouwenfelder, living in The Hague at the time:

'I queued for hours to get some salted endive or some beans. Always that hunger. Even simple German soldiers suffered. Two of them came to search our house. My father had hidden himself just in time.

The boys, for that is what they were, were starving as well. They said that they had received some soup in Amsterdam two days earlier. The next day they were given a slice of black bread and that was all.

With greediness they looked at the little stove where my mother was cooking some potatoes and a piece of cabbage . . .

I remember a man sitting in the window sill of a shop. He sat there all morning gazing around. A few hours later he fell down on the street: dead. No one paid any attention. His corpse was taken away in a car a few hours later.

Sometimes the baker baked bread. The wheel barrows that took the bread to the shops where the bread could be bought with coupons had to be protected by the police. Sometimes the escort

Flying over The ▷
Hague, two Lan-
casters are waved
at by the people.

▷

It was necessary
for policemen to
frisk the volunteers
who had helped to
collect the food to
ensure that
nothing was
stolen or sold on
the black market.

were members of the Landwacht, the Nazi collaborator-police. Gangs of women and children stood waiting for these wheel barrows. It was no longer useful to loot shops, because each and every shop was empty. In the shop windows you saw all kinds of useless things that once were used for publicity and advertising. If a wheel barrow came by the people would attack, grab the policemen, turn over the barrow, steal a few loaves and run away as quickly as possible. Sometimes the police did not do anything to defend the loaves. I think they understood people were getting crazy little by little. But the Nazis would open fire and I know that people were killed on the Vaillantlaan in The Hague. Of course this caused great excitement.

When a looting took place I stayed in the neighbourhood. I was afraid to get into the crowd, so I watched what was happening. I still remember a little rye bread rolling into my direction. I grabbed it and ran away into a laundry on the next street, which looked like a different and utterly quiet place from another world.

I know there were people who broke the wooden floors to have some wood for their fires. The beds would stand on the cross beams. Since food was scarce and bad and since there were terrible draughts in these houses, many people fell ill and died of pneumonia. My mother warned me not to come too close to Mr. or Mrs. so-and-so "for they have lice . . ." Too late, a few days later I was busy scratching myself like mad. Fortunately some spirits of petroleum worked miracles. Lice, a typical proof of dirt and degeneration.

I remember myself begging for food at the railway stations where German conductors and railway personnel were in charge. I tried to sell a watch for a sandwich. German threats chased me away. I tried to find some coal between the rails, but there was little to be found since so many people had been there before me. Then a large locomotive came. From the engineer's

place, a German wearing a typical German cap looked down at me and signed me to come closer. This I did with great hesitation. The man threw an enormous piece of coal at me. For a weak boy like myself it was almost impossible to carry. I put it in a burlap sack I always carried with me and dragged it all the way home. What a surprise it was.

Once houses were being demolished at the edge of the "Sperrgebiet", the prohibited zone. Without a sign, people suddenly rushed to a larger house at the Alexander Gogelweg and started to remove everything made of wood. I managed to get a peice of joist, enough for two or three days warmth.

I wandered about with my friend Chris Roerade with whom I would later join the Dutch Royal Marine Corps. In a flooded meadow we saw an oak wood door floating. We got it out of the water and walked with it for two hours until we finally got home. On our way home we had to defend our treasure from attacks by other boys, wandering about as we did. I recall how I tried to saw down a branchless tree. While doing it we were caught red-handed by the police and taken to the station. They made us stand against the wall for a few hours. From time to time a policeman hit the table with a truncheon. It did not really frighten us as we saw the blow coming, being reflected in the window. We were sent home after receiving a box on the ears; my saw was confiscated.

Below the cafe where our family lived was a gymnasium. I once sneaked in to steal a wooden jumping board which burned very well . . . The climbing pole was a bit more difficult to carry away. But this problem was also solved. First we dragged it into the corridor, making sure they could not see us from the street. In the corridor we sawed it into managable pieces. Later everything made of wood disappeared from the gym. When the war was over only the walls were left.

And then there was less and less. There

Supply und storage of food in The Hague.

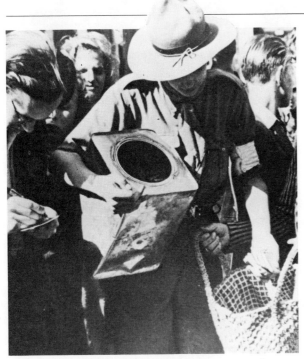

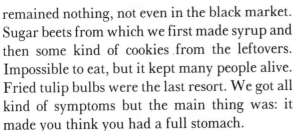

Under the close scrutiny of a colleague, a boy scout distributes recently dropped biscuits.

Watching the 'grocers'.

remained nothing, not even in the black market. Sugar beets from which we first made syrup and then some kind of cookies from the leftovers. Impossible to eat, but it kept many people alive. Fried tulip bulbs were the last resort. We got all kind of symptoms but the main thing was: it made you think you had a full stomach.

And than there came the rumour. Food was to be sent. And believe it or not, it would come by aircraft. And when the planes finally came we saw all kind of odd reactions. Exuberant people waving tablecloths. People standing on roof tops. People rushing about in the street, not being stopped by Germans. People who did not know each other falling into each other's arms crying. Others gazing silently, unable to understand that a miracle was happening, even unable to understand what really was going on.

Anyway, to me it was proof that others cared about us. Rescue was near. Still a lot of people would die but for many more people salvation was coming nearer. Now that I write this, I feel my tears coming back. I cannot explain why.

There was complete surprise when that same day we could taste the first dropped food. Did it come down outside the drop zones? Had it been stolen? I did not know and I could not care less. What an event it was: to taste real black chocolate!! Chocolate is the only thing I remember of that first day. Later we ate biscuits, I believed this was what God himself had for dinner every day. There was "meat and vegetable", egg powder to make enormous egg-pancakes. We tasted dried meat and again chocolate. It was so dark, it seemed almost blue. Even today I love the very dark chocolate most. It brings back a taste to remember forever.

Strangely enough up until a few years ago I would eat excessively. My doctor explained that it possibly was due to the war. Not to know if you would have a meal the next day; to make sure that inside your body you had a reserve for two days to come. It has been locked into my sub-conscience, I think.

I thought the system of distribution was very cleverly arranged. They would not give you too much and the food seemed well balanced. There have been people who literally ate themselves until bursting. They would not be able to decide when their body had had enough food.

And of course we stole like rats, we all did if we could. I know we should not have done so, but we were so very dislocated after the starvation in the West. I think our whole idea of right and wrong had disappeared. It was everyone for himself.'

Like Vrouwenfelder, many people in the famine cities felt this way. Often there were complaints about the long time it took to distribute the food. There were rumours that the people of the distribution authorities first helped themselves before they helped others. People had so little understanding of the enormous problems the Dutch authorities had to face. They did not care that the food had to be first cleaned or that the large quantities had to be divided into smaller one-person portions. The food had been dropped, why was not it distributed now? There were only a few individuals who understood how difficult it was to get the food to the people.

Some people took an active part in the collection and guarding of the dropped food. One of these people was J. van Vliet from Rotterdam, a policeman. Having been involved in the railway strikes, he had been in jail for some time, but he had been put to work in the police force again and was supervising the stockpiles. There he saw how with real Dutch soundness everything was being counted and assorted. He too remembers how sometimes goods were stolen and how great the temptation was to pick up some of the

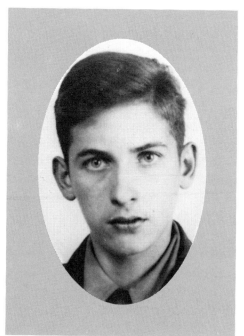

During the drops, young Klaas Schoenmaker managed to get an empty cement bag. When he emigrated to Canada this token of relief went with him.

Food being collected at Vogelenzang under police surveillance.

delicacies waiting to be taken away.

Mrs. Corbet who being a member of the Interior Forces, was involved in the collection of the food that had fallen down near Terbregge, remembers:

'A bag with milk powder burst on impact and I remember how one of the helpers took just a handful of it, got himself water from a ditch, stirred the powder in it and tasted with great care. It was just a little bit, but apparently it was too much for his stomach. He became sick and I felt sorry for him. Then a man in his fifties came towards him, called the poor lad a thief and had him tied against a pole as an example for the others. I do not remember the things I said, but I untied the boy.'

Some people were so weak, that it looked as if they would not live to see the liberation. Someone remembers how her eldest sister of fourteen was so ill that she could not swallow the grey thin soup of the cookhouse. The doctor was helpless. The youngest sister of four had an open wound on her thumb from thumb-sucking and the woman herself was at the end of her rope. Her husband had been arrested and she had no money to buy food on the black market. For people like them, Manna was a rescue at the very last moment.

We should remember how difficult it was for an everyday housewife to get and prepare food. Mrs. E. op den Kelder-Bos was one of these many brave housewives, who accomplished the impossible day after day:

'Our stove had been made from an old tin, once used for paint. I prepared beets that day. Our other food was what we got from the cookhouse, mostly a thin, grey soup. We had no electricity, no gas. We cooked in the tin, using papers from my father's office. We dragged suitcases filled with paper from his office; I still do not understand how I managed, undernourished as I was. We needed two people to keep the stove burning, one to make the pellets and one to handle the pan while the other pushed the pellets inside the stove. Each one had his turn.

The day the aircraft dropped food parcels it was my turn with my eldest sister. We lived at the edge of Rotterdam. Near us the planes came over very, very low and my sister got very curious. She walked to the window to have a look and in panic I called my mother. My mother dragged her back and while doing so she tore the piece of elastic with which my sister held up her slip. Slip on the floor and in spite of all misery we had a terrible laugh. Also of course because we knew that the end of the occupation was near.'

Starvation made people do things that no one would have done under normal circumstances. Who can be blamed for stealing something when he has children at home who can no longer walk for hunger? As a boy Mr. C.W. Pot was present when people were caught during severe controls. They had hidden chocolate inside their socks or had hidden butter underneath their hats. The confiscated goods then were shown to the people. 'One thing I will always remember,' he says. 'During a food transport I walked through the Jericholaan. At a certain moment, an aircraft dropped a little early, it happened more than once and the cargo came down near by. About 25 yards away from us, a large bag with flour crashed in a cloud of dust. When the cloud had gone after a few seconds, the large sack had disappeared . . . Someone had been able to get himself a lot of flour in a very short time, thus assuring himself of plenty of food!'

Mrs. M.A. van Beek from Vlaardingen lived with her husband and three children near the Wilton Shipyard. Sometimes the air raid alarms sounded four times a day. Then they would open the front door to help the people who were looking for cover. They would dress their children with many clothes and wait inside the bathroom. Being under the stairs, this part of the house often survived a hit. 'When the war broke out we were rather wealthy. After the war we had noth-ing; everything we possessed we had swapped for food. When the food droppers came, we all climbed on the roofs, people were waving with orange flags and even clothes that had been tied to broom sticks. We all ran to the field near the Vlaardingen dike, where we saw parcels fall down. And later on: the food! Chocolate, meat and vegetables, even cigarettes for the men. And those biscuits, we had the feeling we would never stop eating again. When I remember myself going to the park to cut a tree to cook, how skinny we were, how the children were starving, I can imagine how the people of Poland feel today! May God give them their freedom too one day.'

It would be untrue to give the idea that everything went well when the food was dropped. In some cases – without knowing it – the crews of the bombers, with all their good intentions, brought pain and sorrow, even death . . . One lady particularly remembers one of the droppings near Terbregge, at the north-east of Rotterdam:

'At the time our family, my husband, my four year old son and I, lived at the Boezemlaan at the

Polish airmen of No. 300 Squadron also came to help the Dutch. L.-r.: w/o Mindykowski (bomb aimer), Sgt Szalacki (mid-upper gunner), Sgt Singer (navigator), Flt/Sgt Wojtowicz (pilot), Sgt Krzak (rear gunner), Sgt Jarozewski (flt. engineer), and Sgt Slonina (wireless operator).

boundary of Rotterdam. I had a crystal-receiver, so I knew that the drops were at hand. I think it was Radio Orange which warned us to stay away from the dropping areas, because people could get hurt. On the first day they dropped near Terbregge I warned several neighbours to be careful. But everything happened so far away from me that I thought nothing could happen. So I went outside to watch the spectacle. I was standing in the middle of a group of mad people, when suddenly bags were dropped. It was all well meant, of course, but within seconds people were lying on the ground, groaning in pains. I was one of the first to be hit. I fell down, and although I tried desperately, I could not get up anymore. Within a split second I was completely paralyzed.

Then other aircraft, possibly confused by the first one, began dropping their food. German soldiers rushed towards us to chase us away. A

Armed with a British stengun and completely ignored by the Dutch bystanders, this elderly German military police soldier 'guards' a truck-load of food near Gouda.

very young German soldier stayed with me and when the drops started again he covered me with his own body. At that instant he was terribly hit himself. I too received a tremendous blow against my right shoulder and fell unconscious. When I came to, the poor German was laying over me dead. I was taken away by ambulance and the German was laid down in the grass. At the St. Franciscus Hospital they saw that my chest had been torn open and that I had concussions everywhere. After ten days, the paralysis disappeared, but I did miss the Liberation. Later I asked everywhere about the German soldier. I would have liked to inform his relatives about what he did for me, but I have never been able to find them. Later they told me that ten other people had been killed. The droppings saved our lives, but we should not forget this happened too.'

In nine other places, people looked at the aircraft with great joy. At Vogelenzang, a village south of Haarlem, people watched the American B-17G Flying Fortresses when they came over on May 1st and dropped Army rations in large boxes over the dropping zone. One of the villag-

ers saw it all happen:

'I lived at the Vogelenzangseweg. From my window on the first floor I could see the large field where they had the 1937 Jamboree. Many parcels came down on that field. I was so angry, when I saw German soldiers collecting the parcels and take them away. They did not seem to be able to give up stealing after all the years they had spent robbing our country. Later people told me that some of the Germans had eaten so much that it had killed them. I must admit that time I found it a wonderful solution to their food problem.'

Some people have very special memories of the food drops. One of them is Mrs. Elsa van Hall-Davis who remembers:

'When the American consulate closed in Amsterdam, I received their American flag. On that famous 1st of May, I went with my four children up to the roof of our flat, laid the American flag down and waited. A plane came over, flew low and tipped its wings, dropped a bag, flew over again and saluted. A grand show. Then with a wheel barrow we brought our sack to the police station. After the liberation, the Germans stole the flag and burned it.'

J.G. Verburgt was a fifteen year old boy when the American bombers flew over his home village Vogelenzang to bring 'chow' to the starving people in the Haarlem area.

'The parcels fell down in the streets. Most of it was flat as a pancake. Other packs fell in the canal, they too had fallen in the wrong place. Everything should have come down at the Jamboree ground, where white clothes formed a large cross. Many people took the parcels directly into their houses, but the next day a house-to-house search was made and everything had to be handed over again.'

Mrs. M.M. Plantjé wrote a poem about the miracle she witnessed near Haarlem:

An airplane skims over the land
The low country called Holland
Country of hunger, persecution and sorrow
In the streets people gaze at the sky
An airplane circles around
The pilots drop their food!
People cry, people cheer to the skies
Food, food, food!

In spite of the pains and the daily sorrow over what would be on the table each day, the Dutch tried to maintain a normal life. Mrs. A.J. Bus still remembers how her father tried to keep the family united and did all he could to provide at least some food in their house in Heemstede:

'During the Hunger Winter my mother was pregnant. We had a horrible lack of food and if we had something we shared it as fairly as possible. My father and eldest brother both were covered with ulcers, because they had had no decent food for weeks. My youngest brother was a six year old infant and I was a girl of thirteen. Mother needed a lot of food for the baby. On 25th April, by the light of a full moon and one candle a healthy baby was born, weighing eight pounds. We had very few clothes for the baby, but thank God she was healthy.

It was silent outside. No one dared to walk on the streets because of the curfew. Sometimes rumours went around; every now and then we read one of the illegal leaflets from the Resistance. Mother was upstairs in bed. We often spent the days in her room. From the window we had clear view over the land around us. And then . . . we heard the sound of heavy aircraft engines. A familiar sound, something that we sometimes listened to for hours when "they" came over to bomb Germany again. But now the sound slowly came closer to us. Suddenly we saw great American bombers. They flew very low from the west to the east. "Something is falling out, they are dropping something. Look, parachutists? No, it looks as if they are dropping bombs." Soon we all knew. "They are dropping food! The Americans are bringing food!" The food came down near Aerdenhout, falling down in the dunes. What a relief, what a miracle it was. I remember myself walking to a nearby shop. A tall, skinny and pale looking child in an old overcoat. Walking on wooden shoes with a pillowcase under my arm. I had the food stamps of the entire family. The baker's shop was open. Inside were large green tins with biscuits. We received a handfull. It was delicious. Soon after this, the Liberation came. After the days of the biscuits, we had the "meat and vegetables" days. The chocolate was excellent. I must admit that the first piece I ate almost made me vomit; my stomach just could not have it anymore. I will never forget the food drops as long as I live. These men saved my life. Last summer, when I was on a holiday in California I told the people what I owe them. My little sister still always has to listen to: "You were not brought by the stork, you came in an American bomber." The hunger could not have been taken much longer. I am still grateful to these young men who saved us at the last moment.'

Jac. W. Kromhout is an old man now. However remembering the food drops it seems to him as if it all happened yesterday:

'After we heard the news through the English radio, we in Vogelenzang lived in great tension.

It was the 1st of May around noon when we saw the aircraft come closer. I do not remember how many they were but one did not have time to count them. They flew incredibly low. Unfortunately something went wrong the first time. The aircraft opened their bomb doors, the food fell down, however it landed at the wrong spot. The pilots dropped their cargo in the bulb fields, thus causing great damage to the bulbs. The actual dropping area was about 1½ miles outside the village. But we did not bother about it; we had the food, that was all that mattered. They were large boxes. In these boxes were rations for the soldiers who fought at the front. Many boxes had been damaged and we were allowed to share them among ourselves. This was done with great gratitude.

The second day when the aircraft came, everything went much better and dropping was done at the right place. This time, no parcels, but sacks were dropped. Inside was flour, butter, eggpowder, dried meat etc. Around the field were many ditches and a lot had fallen into these ditches. At night we went to the ditches with a hook, and every now and then we managed to get something out. The food was collected by Air Raid Wardens, to make sure that everything was distributed fairly among the civilians. The first loads went to the towns. We in the countryside received our share much later, as it was believed that we were reasonable well off compared to the townsmen. This was not true at all.

The third time I remember aircraft was on a Sunday. In the afternoon we went to Church when the priest asked us to help the church warden to hang out the flag. We had just opened the hatch when again aircraft approached. They flew so low that we could easily see the crew from our spot in the steeple. While climbing

In most cases, severly damaged parcels were sent to hospitals and churches.

△

On landing, the boxes were sometimes heavily damaged. This did not hinder the Dutch from often eating it right off the ground.

down again we suddenly heard a loud bang inside the church. When we came on the ground floor we saw that some sacks had fallen straight through the roof between the benches. We opened the sacks and found chocolate, tinned dried meat and a tin with egg powder. Everything was shared as honestly as possible. It was a marvelous event, which I will never forget!'

Mrs. Dedding-Roessen from Vogelenzang still remembers how fantastic it was to see the Flying Fortresses coming over at such a low altitude: 'In the years after I have often spoken about it with other people and I notice that people still remember it so vividly. We talk and say: "Do you remember, first it was boxes, later they dropped sacks. They fell down all over the place even into the Leidse Vaart." Some people had sacks coming straight through the roof of their side-kitchen. They say that some of the pilots mistook the white tulip and daffodil fields near the Zanderij for the dropping zone.

Later these parcels were collected and taken to Haarlem on little barges. I still wonder where the food went. No one is able to tell me. To the

▷ *B-17's over Haarlem.*

B-17's in formation.

Collecting American rations at Schiphol.

hospitals? I will not suggest that no one managed to hide a parcel in his cellar. On the other hand I know about a family with a mother who had given birth only a few days earlier. The midwife had rushed out and grabbed a parcel. I am sure that they badly needed the food in this family. The next day however the husband had to return everything to the authorities. I believe they found a tin with paté and kept it for themselves. These people must have had a wonderful meal together!

My husband was in the Interior Forces and came home from Overveen one evening. When walking along the Vogelenzangseweg he saw a sack in the top of a tree. With great danger – he had a terrible fear for height – he climbed up into the tree and managed to bring the sack down. It turned out to be full of mustard pow-

der. Afterwards we had a big laugh about it. I also remember a young boy stirring in a rain water barrel who suddenly saw peas in the water. After further investigation, he found the drainpipe filled with peas.'

Several times it occurred that aircraft did not drop the food at the intended places. A 'dropping failure' took place not far from the Noord Holland town of Purmerend. On 2nd May the inhabitants heard for the first time about food drops to take place in their neighbourhood. On that day people saw low flying 'Fortresses' flying over their heads. Many people stood waving with white cloths and handkerchiefs. It was a very moving and impressive thing to see. Never before had they seen air parcels. The parcels were dropped in the vicinity of the former milk factory at the Melkweg. The parcels were to be delivered at Doets Inc. at the Gedempte Singel-gracht. Here too efforts were made to steal parcels for private use. On discovery, the people who committed this theft were punished severely. Parts of the parcels were distributed among the people on 7th May. Another part went to various institutions in the town.

Men over 60 were surprised with a tin af meat, women received a bar of chocolate. Apart from the official packages, personal gifts from air crew also came down near Purmerend. In the Overweerse Polder a box filled with candy was found. On the box it read: 'Good morning. For some Holland Child, from an American airman'.

The bombers also flew over Purmerend on May 3rd. Some of the boxes and empty tins were donated after the war to the Museum of Purmerend by the proprietor of the Doets Company.

Unfortunately there were a number of casualties during the drops. In his book *Het Zweedse Wittebrood* ('The Swedish White Bread') the author Nico Scheepmaker tells the story of an anonymous inhabitant of Amsterdam who told what happened to him during the drops near the capital:

> 'On May 3rd around noon, one of the aircraft returning from the drop over Schiphol and flying over Amsterdam released a last container while flying over the Riekwijkerstraat. Without expecting anything people were walking in the street. I happened to be one of them. The container hit my head and this caused serious brain damage, which still bothers me seriously.'

In the same book is a nice story about an event in Utrecht. Mr. A.J. van Kempe wrote about it in a letter to a friend:

> 'Finally the planes skimmed over Utrecht with their food parcels; a magnificent occasion, making people mad with happiness. A very old gentleman stood dancing and screaming and when he was told that the Tommies[1] would not hear him he pointed at a group of about fifty sad-looking Krauts and yelled: "I know, but they do!" Someone else shouted to the Krauts: "Do you see that? This is for us; if something else comes down it is for you!"'

Again we read from the diary of the Rotterdam young man, Kees den Haan whom we heard from previously:

> 'Tuesday May 1st 1945. After a cold night in the hay we went on, direction Piershil. Our search for potatoes was quite successful. I exchanged a black costume for a hectolitre of potatoes and 30 pounds of wheat. Forks and spoons were swapped for 80 pounds of potatoes. After having waved at the Tommies who flew overhead we returned to Klaaswaal. "The grocers" came twice today. In the morning American aircraft in formation; a wonderful view. Once a gunner in the nose of a Flying Fortress waved at us with something that looked like a red-white-blue cloth.'

Wednesday May 2nd 1945. Fifth drop. This morning we returned on our way home. Joop carried 100 pounds of potatoes, which we got asking at every farm, two pounds of wheat and four pounds of peas. I had 260 pounds of potatoes also received through exchange, 30 pounds of wheat – which I used some of to have a delicious bread baked for home – two pounds of peas. This way we reached Puttershoek, where the mayor invited us for lunch. We had the luck of meeting a very nice bargeman who only asked 2½ guilders to take us across the river. Every-

---

[1] For many people Tommies were British as well as Americans.

thing went well and although we were dead tired we came home at 20.00 hours. Fortunately the curfew had been delayed till 21.00 hours.

3rd May 1945. After having had a wash, I went to 't Putje on my bicycle. At 2 o'clock in the afternoon the aircraft came over again. We are getting used to it.

The contents of the parcels were very different. They contained everything: flour, butter, chocolate, cocoa, fat, pepper, salt, bacon, dehydrated eggs, mashed potatoes, cigarettes, tobacco, etc, etc, etc. Next week, the distribution will start. This week we received the eighth bread-ration; next week the ninth and last. After that we will be fed with dropped food and foodstuffs that have been transported by ship and car. The Nieuwe Waterweg-river is open again. OUR SORROWS ARE OVER. WE WILL GET ALL THE FOOD WE NEED! HURRAY!

Friday 4th May 1945. I worked as a roundsman. In the afternoon we went to Heerjansdam where 30 pounds of potatoes were still waiting for me. In the "Pieterman" I exchanged a dress from Aunt Miep for eight pounds of wheat. She was delighted. I also received two bottles of milk.

AT NINE O'CLOCK WE RECEIVED THE NEWS THAT WESTERN NETHERLANDS, DENMARK AND WESTERN GERMANY HAVE SURRENDERED!!!

On May 8th our names were written down to work to deliver parcels to families in distress. We were driven to the Hofdijk in a Jeep and then went in the direction of Terbregge by car. Over there, I and the others who delivered parcels received a delicious plate with hot food. After that I worked at the dropping zone for another hour. At seven I went home with half a loaf of bread.

10th May 1945. Pathfinders with five wheel barrows went to the town hall. There we received instructions, and with three other boys I took a wheel barrow to bring parcels to distressed families. Each of us received pea flour for it. We delivered in the western part of Rotterdam and in a part of Delfshaven. We made many people happy that day. Everyone received four little sacks for 75 cents, along with butter, the latter coming from the aircraft and given out

Many people will vividly remember the meat and vegetables.

free of charge. We did not get any food so I went home for two sandwiches. We saw a lot of very bad situations. In the Derde Schansstraat we found an eldery couple so underfed that they were no longer able to go to the toilet. One can imagine the hygienic situation. At 5.30 hour we helped our last customer and returned to the Hofdijk. There everything lies packed in tins and I was astonished to see the variety of the articles.'

From May 1st American bombers were also used to drop food over the occupied territory. Again we are aware many years after the drops what emotional memories of the food bombardments have remained. Tom Lammers, currently living in Bosch en Duin still remembers how close the liberation seemed to come to his native town of Hilversum:

'From early September 1944 – "Mad Tuesday"[1] – we expected the liberation to be a matter of days or weeks. The Allies had reached our country now and large parts (the south) had been liberated. The situation in the west though grew worse each day; now hunger came to our doorstep. Thanks to some relatives who were farmers we had been able to stock some wheat and rye. From March 1945 however we had to use these stocks and shared it with friends and

neighbours who did not have anything after the Central Kitchen had failed to feed them. On March 13th we received the first loaf of white bread from the baker using a special coupon. He had been able to bake this bread thanks to the flour that had been donated by the Swedish Red Cross. The bread tasted delicious and I am sure that in many families battles were fought over the last bit of bread that was left. Although there was no more electricity, thanks to my crystal receiver I was able to receive Radio Orange very well. Thus I could supply the neighbourhood with the latest news. This was how we knew that there was a battle going on at the Veluwe area on 16th and 17th April. We saw the German retreating from Hilversum. On April 19th there was fighting around Amersfoort and we knew that the liberation was only a matter of days, even hours. At that time we heard the first rumours about the possible food supply drops that were being discussed and arranged with the Germans still occupying Western Holland.

---

[1] 'Mad Tuesday' was Tuesday 5th September 1944, when large groups of Germans and Dutch Quislings left the country for Germany after the rumour had been spread that Allied forces were moving north so quickly that the liberation of Holland would be a matter of days, even hours.

At last it happened on May 2nd. In Hilversum on the Westerheide along the railroad from Hilversum to Bussum between Hilversum and Crailo, the first food drops took place. What a feast! Food was also dropped on the other side of the railroad in the "Stad en Lande van Gooiland" area, where now you can find the NOS-TV studios. In a way it was a bit dangerous to stand there cheering, for the heavy tins could hit you very unpleasantly. Fortunately everything went well and I never heard that any accidents happened. It was a tremendous psychological thrill. The mere idea that the Allies would put an end to the food emergency and soon they would begin to distribute the "Manna" was enough to keep courage and hold on for a while. According to my notes I helped the baker, a relative, to empty the tins filled with biscuits which had been supplied to the grocers etc. They were "army green" rectangular tins containing about 20 pounds of biscuits. It was British Army food. Many of the biscuits had been damaged and become crumbs, but two cared? The Municipal Central Kitchen was working much better by that time and supplied us with a kind of porridge, made from the biscuits crumbs and dried milk which had been donated by the Swedish Red Cross as well. It was the best porridge I ever ate.'

Mrs. K. Philippo-Gasch had rather unpleasant neighbours during the war. She lived Rijksstraatweg 32. At number 34 the Germans had their billets and an office. The soldiers belonged to a unit that was stationed along the Bekslaan in Vogelenzang. From this site they launched theur V-I rockets from time to time. In the other house next door Germans had also been billeted. During the early morning of May 1st a German approached her and said: 'Today the Americans will come and drop supplies for you. We have to stay inside; we are not even allowed to meddle with your affairs!' Mrs. Philippo remembers how the first bombers arrived over Vogelenzang and chose the wrong dropping zone. The food parcels skimmed over her house and fell down in the field in front of the Leidse Vaart canal. The next day they did not repeat this mistake and dropped the supplies along the Vogelenzangseweg.

It must have been very tempting for the starving townspeople to take something of the fallen delicacies home. Though it came down from a low altitude many tins, boxes and bags had been severely damaged. Butter, sugar, coffee and flour had been crushed at Schiphol. Therefore the food had to be cleaned before distributing it among the population. Someone who once worked at Schiphol told about the variety of damaged parcels in *Trouw* newspaper of 28th April 1965:

'Passing by, one would take a clot of liver pie and eat it . . . Many tins were torn when they hit the remains of the hangars. Rice and pineapple sluiced around. Everywhere at Schiphol brown stains of sugar could be seen. The smell of coffee from burst bags entered your nose. There was bacon, there were sausages laying about. After the last squadron had left – recognizable by the red tail lights – Schiphol was covered with thousands of small and large parcels. When leaving, one was searched: who did not behave like a starving animal at that time? The damaged supplies went to the hospitals immediately. The large blocks of concrete had caused quite a bit of damage. Detectives were searching all the time. When we left, we had to go through a grove. One of the lads had hidden a packet of tea underneath a cart. He was caught at the checkpoint and kicked off the field for good.'

▷ *You took a blob of liver-pie and licked your hands.*

▽ *A 388th Bomb Group* B-17.

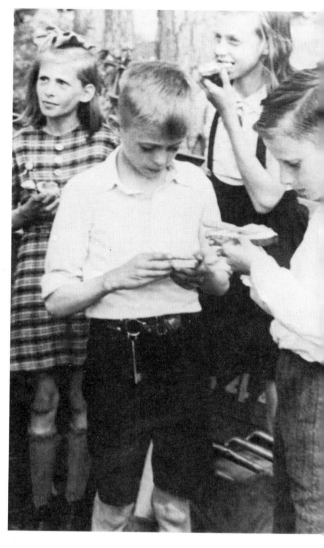

Something of the great joy can be understood from what was written in the *Dagblad voor Noord-Holland* newspaper of May 4th 1945:

'Wednesday Alkmaar experienced a day of tension, a day that will not be easily forgotten. Tuesday, the news went from mouth to mouth that the next morning Allied aircraft would drop food parcels over the airfield at Bergen. The food parcels would be collected by the Germans and put at the disposal of Mr. Kamp JD, who had also been responsible for the distribution of the Swedish gifts in the northern part of Noord-Holland. Already at seven o'clock hundreds of people went to the Hoeverweg and the Bergerweg. The roads leading to the airfield had already been blocked by the Marechaussee-police, while at the airfield the industrious fire brigade of Alkmaar and the men of the Economic Police were present under command of Mr. Kamp, waiting to transport the parcels as quickly as possible to the central point, the storehouses of Holmuller Ltd. at the Voordam.

At half past nine the first aircraft, about ten, appeared over the airfield after having flown over Alkmaar, this time as birds of peace. After an hour these aircraft were followed by many tens of others. In Alkmaar it was as busy as during a football game at normal times. People had gathered on hundreds of roofs, many of them with binoculars. However they established that no parcels were being dropped, and they were convinced that they had missed the view of the drop. Nor were parcels seen to be dropped at the airfield. It turned out that the aircraft had in fact dropped their valuable and welcome cargo somewhere else.

At approximately half past one, about thirty aircraft appeared, coming in from the sea. They dropped about 1500 parcels each having a weight of about 40 pounds. These were safely stored in the Holsmuller storehouses at 6 o'clock. As Mr. Kamp told us, the distribution will take another few days. First of all the total amount is not enough for the entire north of North Holland province. In the second place the parcels contain forty different articles. The damaged parcels were immediately sent to the Church Organization for distribution. In the Schermer polder about fifty parcels had also fallen and were collected by the Marechaussee-police. It happened that a wealthy farmer

On 7th May, Lancaster MG '*H for Harry' of No. 7 Squadron* (PFF) *dropped markers and food. On the bomb bay doors, it read 'Wilson's Express Service', on the nose* 'VE *Taxi Service'. In the cockpit, the chief taxi driver, Flt/Lt J. Wilson.*

had not hesitated to hide some parcels in his hay stack. A person like this is a shame to his standing.

After what has been achieved, it proves that everything possible is being done to make sure that the people in the Occupied Territory do not starve. The missions will be continued daily. The most gladdening thing is that the Allies have come to an agreement with the Germans, making it possible to unload ships with food at the docks of Rotterdam and to allow transportation of the food along roads that have been cleared by the oppressor. Thanks to this, thousands can still be saved from starvation. A bugbear has been taken away from us now.'

After the leaflet *De Vliegende Hollander* (The Flying Dutchman) had been dropped over our country on April 20th, the news about the floodings the Germans had caused in the west of the country became known. It became obvious that the people should not expect armed action to liberate the west. On April 30th, one day after the first food drops, *De Vliegende Hollander* reported:

'On Sunday 29th April RAF bombers, by command of the Allied Supreme Headquarters for the first time dropped food over Western Holland at Waalhaven, Ypenburg, Valkenburg and Rijswijk race track. The zones had been blocked and were strongly guarded. The food was to be distributed within the normal system by the National Bureau Food Supply in Wartime. Do not go to the drop zones. Do give all your help to assure fair distribution!'

On Wednesday 2nd May 1945 *De Vliegende Hollander* again reported about the food drops, this time in a German article: *Nachrichten für die deutschen Truppen* (News for the German Forces). On the back page of this leaflet was a report about the negotiations between Allied and German representatives:

'Food for the Netherlands.

An agreement between Allies and Germans.

London 2nd May – The Allied Headquarters yesterday reported that Monday, Allied and German representatives came together and agreed to arrangements with respect to the supply of food to the Dutch population in Occupied Holland by air, by land and by sea. Present from Allied side were: Lieutenant-General Bedell Smith, Chief of Staff Supreme Allied Headquarters (chairman); Major-General Suslaparov, representing the Soviet-Union; Major-General Strong of the Allied Headquarters; Major-General De Guingand, Chief of the Staff 21st Army Group; Major-General Galloway, Commander Holland District, Lieutenant-General Prince Bernhard, Commander Netherlands Forces; Brigadier Williams, 21st Army Group (secretary) and naval, army and air force officers and interpreters. The German delegation was under the leadership of Reichskom-

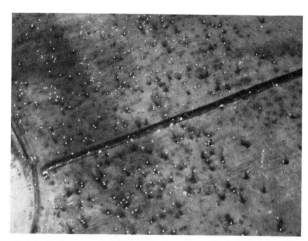

Schiphol covered with food. The dark spots show the force with which the sacks hit the ground.

agreed that the supply ships would put into Rotterdam, where the Germans would meet the ships at an arranged point and safely escort them into the docks. The Germans have cleared one major road for transport of food over land. The supply by lorries will start today (2nd May) with an amount of 1,000 tons. The Algemeen Nederlands Persbureau Press Agency reports that the negotiations took place in a village between the Canadian and German lines.'

It must be said in all honesty that a far more important message – as far as the Allies were concerned – was printed on the front page of the *Vliegende Hollander*: 'HITLER IS DEAD.'

The Allied as well as the Dutch government in London and the authorities in the Occupied Areas were afraid that some people would try to bring the food onto the black market. Therefore it said on the front page of the leaflet:

'Great quantities of food are now being supplied to Western Holland. Some thousands of tons already have been dropped. Now too food is arriving by ship and the first transport columns by road

B-17's heading for Ypenburg on 1st May 1945. The dark horizontal stripes on the tail fins indicate they are 388th Bomb Group.

missar Seyss-Inquart and consisted of officers of the German navy, army and air force as well as civil experts. General Smith read the general propositions for food supply to the Dutch population and received permission in principle from the Germans. Mixed commissions were formed to work out the particular aspects of the plan. For the supply of food by aircraft, ten drop zones were pointed out. Over these zones Allied airplanes would not be fired upon between 0700 and 1500. For the supply by ship, it was

A food collection squad standing between burlap cement bags filled with food.

have started on May 2nd. All this food will be distributed by the Dutch authorities through the usual distribution channels. The Dutch government appeals to the population: do all to help assure a fair distribution of the food. Do not engage yourselves in black marketeering and save the food for those who are starving!'

On 3rd and 4th May an appeal was repeated briefly, with the addition:

'Difficult as it might be – do not involve yourselves in premature demonstrations. The appearance of Allied lorries does not yet mean that you are being liberated. The government requests: self-control!'

The last issue of the *Vliegende Hollander* appeared on May 10th 1945. Once again the editors paid attention to the food drops. A Sunday dispatch cartoon showed a small group of British pilots with in their midst a moustached airman, making wild gestures, reporting with pathos: 'Then I dived down to 300 feet and released 2,000 loaves of bread!'

A historical drawing it was. With it the fairy tale of the Swedish loaves raining down was born. And the fairy tale remains alive today. Nico Scheepmaker shows this in his book *Het Zweedse Wittebrood* ('The Swedish White Bread') and even the poet, Cees Buddingh', from Dordrecht did not escape the myth in his des-

cription of hundreds of Dutch people, seeing with their own eyes 'how the loaves came falling down' . . .

With a reluctance that was in violent contrast with the sometimes gushing manner in which German victories had been previously described, the newspaper *Het Volk* reported on May 4th about the Allied food supplies:

'Food by air, sea and road.

The Hague, May 2nd. In the matter of food supply to the Netherlands by air, sea and road, an agreement has been signed between German and Allied representatives. The supply by air will be daily between 7 and 3 o'clock. During this time Allied aircraft will drop parcels without any German impediment. The food supplies to Rotterdam will be escorted by the Kriegsmarine. The German delegation was headed by the Commissioner for the Occupied Dutch Territory, Reichsminister Dr. Seyss-Inquart. The Allied delegation was headed by the Chief of Staff of the Allied Supreme Commander, Lieutenant-General W.E. Smith.'

Two columns left of this little article are occupied by a two column report: 'The Führer has died in combat. Great-Admiral Dönitz successor. We will continue to fight against Bolshevism!'

On 1st May, the first Allied ship carrying food supplies steamed up the Nieuwe Waterweg River under German escort. The people of Maassluis showed their gratitude by presenting the crew of the first ship with an enormous wreath.

The *Radio-Orange* reports that same day were as follows:

'20,000 tons of food by road. Allied aircraft drop 30 million rations. Shortly ships to Rotterdam.

According to Anep, a complete truce has been agreed at a certain point between the German and Canadian lines. There Canadian and English drivers take their food which they have transported for the starving Dutch population since May 2nd. Three meetings between German and British military have taken place, however on May 1st these consultations have come to an end. Present were the Commander of the 1st Canadian Corps and the German Commander Blaskowitz.

On May 2nd, at a few minutes before seven, the first Canadian cars rumbled to the discharge posts. There the Canadians found Dutch officials, policemen and some men of the ss. The discharge was started immediately, however it was noticed that the Dutch workers did not have much stamina. Therefore they got their first taste of biscuits and tinned fish. Each transport columm was prececed by a Jeep with a white flag. Each car had a number and drove to a tree carrying the same number. There the food was unloaded Further transportation is done by Canadian lorries. The Canadians have made 200 three-ton lorries available, including the necessary fuel. During the afternoon, already 1,000 tons of food had been delivered. A total of 30,000 tons will be taken to the West this way. In a while ships will follow to Rotterdam. Today 800 tons were dropped. It is the intention to fly 30 million rations to our country.'

In the province of Utrecht it turned out to be necessary to appeal officially through the Provincial Commissary for Food in order to make sure that no people took advantage of the sometimes chaotic scenes on and around the dropping zones:

'Appeal to the citizens.

As you know many food packages have not been dropped at the official dropping zones by the aircraft. As a result the packages did not get where they should. For this reason I appeal to everyone to make sure that these lost packages are handed over to the police. They who know addresses where parcels haven been hidden are urgently requested to report this to the police or to the Bureau of the Provincial Commissary for Food, Nieuwe Gracht 135, Utrecht.

Food collectors waiting to be taken to Schiphol. In the background is the Amsterdam Olympic Stadium of 1928.

Citizens, remember it is your DUTY as good Dutchmen to make sure that these packages come where they belong, in order to assure a just and fair distribution. You will understand that almost each parcel has been damaged on impact. Therefore they all have to be opened and sorted out. In spite of many helpers, this will take some time. Therefore it will not be possible until the middle of next week to distribute the packages. The Provincial Commissary for Food in Utrecht.'

On May 6th an 'Amsterdam News bulletin' appeared in the *Parool* newspaper, saying that during the same week the distribution of food would commence:

'We are able to inform our readers that during this week 100 grams of butter or margarine and 50 grams of chocolate will be handed out. Further it is announced that for one coupon tinned meat, bacon or sausages will be available. Tinned vegetables will be available as well. The authorities assume that already on Wednesday or Thursday the distribution will begin. The packages which have been damaged during the droppings and which contain contents which must be distributed quickly will be distributed among orphanages and people who suffer from oedema.'

In a following chapter we will read how the distribution of Allied and Swedish supplies was done so quickly. We will read also about the stage of starvation seen by an Allied team of inquiry in the cities of the former 'Fortress Holland'.

The London *Daily Herald* appeared on 8th May, the last day of the operation, under the headline:

'HOLLAND WAS SAVED JUST IN TIME
Only a few realized how really serious was the urgency of rushing food to the Dutch and how close the Netherlands came to a catastrophe from which it might never have recovered.

Eisenhower knew how serious the situation was, which is why he called the Food Conference of April 30th, four days after the last rations had been distributed.

Dutch civilians attending that conference said the sight of this fleet of planes showering food down was a mighty boost to morale, even though distribution was very difficult.

The food reached the Dutch only just in time.'

The RAF and the USAAF, founded to bring destruction, both ended their participation in this global war by bringing not only food, but also hope to the people of a small and fearful nation. A nation partially flooded, a nation with the scars of death and destruction. The help from the RAF and the USAAF, as well as the help from the governments of Switzerland and Sweden and the long convoys of Allied lorries, came just in time. Although the aid from the two neutral countries was a very great help indeed, the food supplies flown in and driven in turned out to be the last resource available in preventing mass starvation.

We should realize however that the supply drops would have been practically impossible if the Germans had tried to prevent it. The terrible losses, the undoubtedly strong protests from public opinion in the United States and the Commonwealth would have forced the Allies to abandon the operation as it had been planned. Fortunately for both the Allies and the Dutch population, the German forces in Western Holland had been cut off from what remained of the Great German Empire. Communications had been impossible ever since the Canadians and the Poles had rushed North.

The German forces in Western Holland still numbered almost 120,000 men. They had suffi-

Sunday Dispatch. MAY 6, 1945

'Then I dived down to 300 feet and released 2,000 loaves of bread!'—*By Roland Davies*

This cartoon might probably be the reason why some Dutch still believe that loaves of bread were dropped rather than food parcels.

cient light arms, machine guns, guns and explosives. The Dutch Interior Forces resistance counting approximately 17,000 men, half of them armed, would have been no match for the Germans. The Allies did not have enough troops to conquer West Holland without terrible destruction and the Germans could inudate practically any place they wanted to. Therefore the only possibility to save the population was to convince the Germans that there was no alternative but to surrender, or at least to convince them that they should allow food aid by the Allies.

On 7th May at 22.00 hours Radio Resurgent Netherlands announced that during the following day the distribution of food dropped by the RAF (and the USAAF) would continue:

> 'Every effort will be made to bring 300 tons of coal daily to the communal kitchens to prepare the meals. It is intended to increase this figure to 4,000 tons daily. Our own mines in the province of Limburg will supply the coal. It is hoped that soon 2,000,000 litres of paraffin will be made available to the suffering population of the Western Netherlands for cooking purposes. The Relief Corps and the Red Cross have not yet left, but will be ready to begin their work shortly.'

Fortunately, the situation turned out not to be as serious or dangerous as had been expected only a few weeks earlier. Brigadier Wedd, the Deputy Director of Civil Affairs, reported what his Civil Affairs officers had seen when they entered the western part after the Germans surrendered:

> 'The picture appears to be that while a

state of actual general starvation as feared had not been reached at the time of the entry of our troups, the state of food supplies would indicate that this catastrophe had only been avoided by a matter of two or three weeks. Conditions appear to vary in several cities with Rotterdam as probably the worst.'

In spite of the tremendous job that was done by the Allies, between 100,000 and 150,000 cases of starvation oedema were reported in the whole B-2 area. About 20,000 people actually starved to death in spite of all help. It is almost impossible to realize that this happened in a once fertile and prosperous country. Had the Allied food come later, however, it would have cost many more lives. Possibly the fear expressed by the Dutch Government in exile in London would have been realized and there would have been a liberation of only corpes...

Kees den Haan became busier and busier after the liberation. We have already read of how he and other boy scouts went to the houses of the worst cases of famine to bring little parcels with food. In his diary he wrote:

'12th May 1945. This morning I reported at the Schiedamsesingel and received my identification as a member of the Youth Help. After that I went to the River Police, but without a permit I was not allowed te enter the grounds to offer my assistance. At Thomsen they did not need any help either. I had more luck a St. Job's where I was accepted with five other boy scouts. At that place, the food stocks from the air drops were discharged, sorted and taken to the grocery shops by cart or car. I went with them all day. In the afternoon they served us a plate of delicious pea soup with bacon. The three of us ate a tin of bacon which tasted delicious. After that we could not eat anything more. They also gave us biscuits and chocolate. By car we mainly worked at Overschie and Hillegersberg and when I came home in the evening I had some sugar and chocolate for the people at home.

Today I had a very good day. It has been extremely hot this week and it not easy to work in the hot sun all day. But the food is marvellous. After the last load I went to the Westersingel to report again. Everywhere in the windows little lamps and candles were burning, for THE BLACK-OUT HAS BEEN ABOLISHED STARTING TODAY!

It was a nice view. A street organ and an orchestra played. A large fire was burning and young people and Canadians were dancing around it. In one word: it was very comfortable, just like before the war.

Today we received our first parcel from the air. We got three ounces of butter, 1 tin of cheese, 1 coupon for egg powder and three bars of chocolate. It tasted more than delicious. One spoon of egg powder and two spoons of water made a wonderful fried egg.

Tomorrow too I have to be at St. Job all day. It is amazing what has been piled up there. Tins of sugar, tea, coffee, cheese, bacon, chocolate, egg powder and so on.

This week three coupons have been disignated for half a loaf of bread, but unfortunately we could not get bread today.

Sunday 13th May 1945.

We got up early and ate pancakes. This time we fortunately did not have to use sugar beet pulp and we also made ourselves a fried egg. We then ate a plateful of a gigantic meal, even without any bread. At 9 o'clock I arrived at St. Job and came back home at 5. We took food to Overschie, Hillegersberg and Terbregge. In the afternoon we got delicious soup and some bacon. There was enough chocolate but unfortunately I could not take with me what I could not eat. It was very hot indeed and we drank a lot. When we left, my friend and I both got five cigarettes.'

Watched by Dutchmen and Germans (above), the B-17*'s fly over the destroyed runways of Schiphol Airport (below).*

Liberated and hungry

While Lancasters and Flying Fortresses continued dropping food, on Monday May 7th at 08.30 the first Allied troops drove through the German lines into the West of the country. Escorted by a German military vehicle, British Humber armoured cars drove to Hilversum, Amersfoort, Baarn and Utrecht.

The next day, VE day, the Second World War in Europe officially came to an end. Still many men would be killed by the war after that date: Canadians, Britons, Dutchmen and Germans. All over the country however, the flags could now fly. People danced and cheered. Allied vehicles were buried under flowers and people. Dutch girls embraced the merry Allied soldiers who were of a completely different nature than the field grey Germans. In some cases they were the same girls who had embraced Heinrich, Johann or Karl only a few weeks before.

The broken grey Wehrmacht cars had vanished from the streets. Chevrolets, GMC's, Fords, tiny Jeeps and Austins, all painted green, driving on real petrol, now raced along the roads.

The sight of thousands of cheering Dutchmen unfortunately gave the Canadians the wrong impression of the state of health of the population. The ones who did not appear in the streets were the elderly, the sick, the weak and the

After the liberation cars from the 'Food Flying Squad' appeared on the streets. These vehicles were originally sent to the British during the Blitz by the Americans. After the liberation, Queen Elizabeth of Great Britain put the 'Food Flying Squad' at the disposal of the Dutch. Note the barefooted children.

In May 1945, Sir Jack Drummond, leader of a specially equipped Nutrition Committee entered the Western Provinces. He first thought that the situation in Holland was infinitely better than expected, but revised his opinion later.

dying. At home under blankets they silently waited for help to be sent. As indicated in a previous chapter, the Canadians thought that the situation of the starving Dutch was not as bad as they had been told. Sir Jack Drummond who was in charge of an Allied food committee reported, completely mistaken, but from his standpoint understandably so: 'People are thin indeed. However one cannot say that they are starving. The situation tends to be much better than we could have expected.' Mislead by this information, General De Guingand as well reported that the wrong idea had been given about the situation in Holland. He was of the opinion that the Dutch government in London had for obvious reasons greatly exaggerated the situation in the hope of receiving as much help as possible.

The Commander of Holland District, General Galloway, who had participated in the negotiations with the Germans, sent completely different information to his superiors. Galloway looked beyond the rows of cheering people, when he wrote in his report to Allied Supreme Headquarters:

'All we saw were the healthy and the reasonably healthy. The cheering and the flags misled us, not the Dutch government. The country has been looted, fertile country has been affected by sea water. The people in the big cities can only buy food on the black market at incredibly high prices. The average loss of weight is over 40 pounds. Half of the population in the big cities suffers from undernourishment, 15% lives at the brink of starvation. Only 35% is reasonably healthy.'

Galloway's report forced Drummond to review his opinion. He made another trip through the liberated West. He was fair enough to withdraw his previous comments. In a new report, he compared the inhabitants of Rotterdam, The Hague and Amsterdam with the victims of the concentration camps. In the official SHAEF report, it reads further:

'Fall of body weight was progressive and rapid. All the characteristic signs of calorie-defiency appeared: undue fatigue on moderate exercise, feeling cold, mental listlessness, apathy, obsessions with thoughts of food etc. In the beginning men especially were affected. It is easy to write now that each person got 400 calories a day. In practice it was quite another thing. Each Thursday there was published the list of the coupon numbers that were valid for the next week's food. One planned to divide that food over the week. The ordinary person, however, often consumed in two or three days all that was given for the whole week. Consequently there was an enforced fast for four days until the next rations were available. This seriously aggravated the situation. People sought food everywhere in the streets and the surrounding countryside. Anything edible was picked up in this way and they were lucky who found a potato or two or a handful of greens.

In January 1945 the first cases of hunger oedema appeared and were admitted to the hospitals. Soon the numbers multiplied. Little relief could be offered to these patients. Even in the hospitals there was little food. The nurses and physicians worked day and night without supplementary rations. Their menu, for example, was: one slice of bread and one cup of tea substitute for breakfast; two potatoes, a little bit of vegetables and some watery sauce for lunch; one or two slices of bread with a cup of coffee substitute and a plate of soup for dinner. This soup was frequently made with sugar beets by the Communal Kitchen. For hospital patients, however, there was a little more food available, so something could be done for them. In February, however, so many came complaining of starvation, that the hospitals could not admit them all.

In several towns starvation-hospitals were established. With the help of the Underground Forces schools were transformed into hospitals, complete with beds, blankets, sheets and other necessities. Food too was brought in by the Underground Forces. In spite of all these efforts enough beds could not be made available. The patients admitted were treated until they were able to walk and then were discharged. In many cases this remission was only temporary. There was always a waiting list of patients waiting for admission and many of these

Famine-stricken cities:

○ *over 500,000 inhabitants*
◉ *100,000 - 500,000 inhabitants*
• *40,000 - 100,000 inhabitants*

1. *The Hague*
2. *Rotterdam*
3. *Amsterdam*
4. *Haarlem*
5. *Utrecht*
6. *Leiden*
7. *Hilversum*
8. *Alkmaar*

were those who had been previously treated. In addition considerable help was given through polyclinics. Those who had lost 25% of their normal body weight received supplementary rations. At the beginning of 1945 this amounted to 400 grams of bread, 500 grams of beans per day and some milk, when it was available. Later on this supplement was reduced to 400 grams of bread alone, and it was only given when the decrease of weight was as great as 35% of 40%; too many people had reached the level of -25%.

In view of the large number of starving people, these polyclinics for starvation patients were set up in several towns. Here examinations were made. Weights were taken and the patients inspected for oedema. Urine was examined to differentiate hunger-oedema from the frequently occurring nephritis. Then the worst patients received a coupon for one meal per day from the IKB (The Inter-Church Bureau) for two or three weeks. If the patient was too ill to walk to the canteen, the meal was delivered to the home by volunteer helpers. These volunteers were mostly children of about 14 years, because adults were in real danger of being "picked up" by the Germans for enforced work in the defence areas. There was little opportunity to collect data at these polyclinics because of the pressure of work: for example at Rotterdam 600 people were examined by 4 doctors each morning. After the liberation many more such polyclinics were set up. When more food came available their aid became more effective.

In spite of this local organization and effort, conditions became worse. People dropped from exhaustion in the streets

The crew of 42-97982. Standing l.-r.: McMahon (gunner), Church (ball gunner), Korol (flt engineer), Burke (radio operator), Eaton (tail gunner), and Starks (gunner). Kneeling l.-r.: Chrystal (pilot), Slusher (co-pilot), Bonneville (navigator).

and many died there. Often people were so fatigued that they were unable to return home before curfew; so they hid in barns or elsewhere to sleep and died there. Older people who lacked the strength to go searching for food stayed at home in bed and died. The worst cases were hidden in the homes and being unknown to the physicians, could not be treated. Famine took its course with all consequences. Vermin became common; there was no soap. Frequently there was no water, gas or electricity. Many people had skin infections, and frequently, abcesses and phlegmones.

The exact number of hunger-oedema patients remained unknown. Only an estimate can be made from data from some of the larger towns. In May 1945 some 200,000 people needed additional food.'

Five crew members of LS 'L for Love'. L.-r.: Pat Russel, Paddy Kirrane, Douglas Hunt, George Pitkin and John Sheppard. 'L for Love' flew no less than 84 operations, 3 Manna missions, and 3 Exodus flights, bringing British POW's home.

The famine reached its greatest intensity during the four weeks preceeding the final liberation on May 7th. As told by some of the witnesses earlier, the countryside was 'flooded' with townspeople trying to buy, find or steal something to eat. The cold winter and the declining strength of the people made the search for food increasingly difficult. Many died from exhaustion by the roadside. The calorie-rate had fallen appall-

The crew of one of the 388th Bomb Group's Flying Fortresses. Standing l.-r.: T/s Cooperman (radio operator), 1st Lt Burris (pilot), 2nd Lt Walters (bombardier), 2nd Lt Cathcart (navigator), 2nd Kish (co-pilot), T/s Forgerson (flt engineer). Kneeling l.-r.: Sgt Hasak (gunner), Sgt Hardersen (tail gunner), Sgt Wood (ball gunner).
B-17's of 388th Bomb Group on their way to Schiphol. ▽

ingly since October 1944. At that time it was approximately 1,400 calories. In February 1945, it had fallen down to 1,000, and in April it had been reduced to 800 calories or less. The official ration intake however was reduced at a much more rapid rate. To maintain total intake levels at the figures quoted, it was necessary to use stocks of food which had been hidden away, and to make frequent forage trips into the more fertile provinces in the eastern part of the country. In addition sugar beets and tulip bulbs were widely eaten during the six months prior to the liberation. This represented additional food sources not normally used. Also the development of large central kitchens in several areas accounted for a more economical use of food and fuel. These factors however were only of influence for a short period of time. Stocks of hidden food were rapidly used. Foraging expeditions became more difficult and longer. The Germans became more inclined to confiscate food obtained in this fashion. In addition, this average food intake did not apply to all people. The elderly could not forage for food. The very poor could not buy or exchange for food. The occupants of institutions who received only the minimal legal rations were very much worse off than the average individual. The situation deteriorated rapidly in the period immediately after the German surrender and the intake of food from all sources daily was quickly reduced to extremely low levels. In some instances it fell down to 500 to 600 calories!

The results of the physical examinations at the time revealed that the reduced food intake had already produced evidence of starvation. Less than half of the people examined in the representative surveys presented an appearance which could be considered as normal. Most could be classified as thin, some very thin, and a few emanciated. The report estimated that weight loss averaged about 15-20% of total body weight. Hungeroedema appeared in January 1945 and by May 1945 had affected an estimated 10% of the city populations. Menstrual irregularities, or amenorrhea were reported in no less than 50% of all women examined. The groups with the largest risk of dying were males, those at either age extremes and those from less prosperous classes.

The first acquaintance with the Allied food was

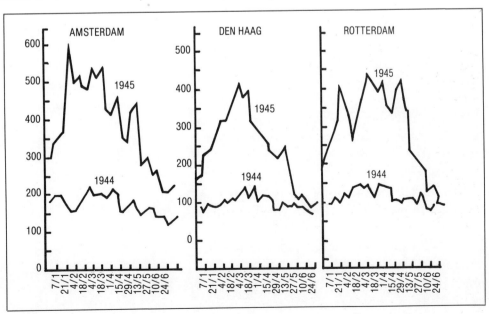

Death rate in the three largest cities in the western region between 7 January and 1 July 1945. As a comparison the death rate for the same period in 1944 is also given. (From: Burger, Drummond and Sandstead; Malnutrition and Starvation in Western Netherlands.)

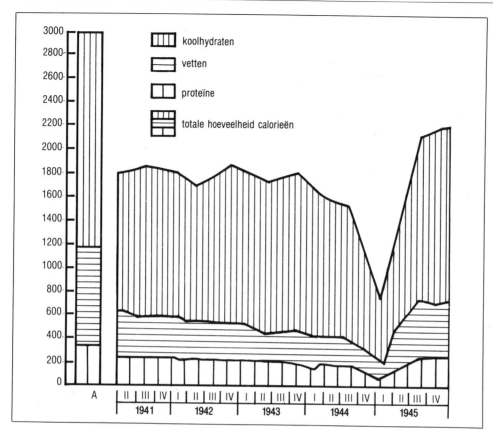

Average disribution of food in Carbohydrates, Fats and Proteins per quarter in West Netherlands from early 1945 till the end of 1945.
A: Desired intake level.
(From: Burger, Drummond and Sandstead; Malnutrition and Starvation in Western Netherlands.)

a rather shocking one for many people. Someone from Amsterdam wrote: 'A Canadian soldier gave me a cigarette. I will never forget the brand was "Woodbine".

Greedy I puffed. It seemed to me as if Amsterdam was turning around me entirely. I got so dizzy that I had to hold myself on a lantern post . . .'

Someone else remembered the first bacon he ate: 'It tasted incredibly good, I agree. But after an hour, the fat bacon made me so sick that I was running from the toilet and back like mad.'

It was a disappointment for many people that they had to wait so long for the food that had been dropped by the British and the Americans. People were not aware of the problems the distribution officials had to face. So signs of discontent and suspicion were everywhere. 'The high gentlemen are probably too busy eating', was a

complaint that often was heard. How untrue this all was!

In the first place, it had been an enormous task to take the food from the dropping zones to the collection centres with the few means of transportation available. There was nothing but horse drawn carts, barges and push-carts. Besides, all the food had to be sorted. Flour, coffee, meat, sugar, everything had been dropped together. Although the aircraft had flown dangerously low, much food had been damaged when it hit the ground.

An eyewitness remembered: 'It was a terrible mess at Ypenburg. The entire airfield had been covered with sacks. Some sacks had fallen in the many little ditches. Sacks filled with peas had burst. There was butter on the grass. Peas and beans had been spread as if it had snowed. Tins had been smashed. It was one big pulp of food, as far as the eye could see.' After the food had been stored it was necessary to clean it from grass, mud, sand and duck-weed.

The bulk of the food caused another problem. What would a hungry person do with 2 pounds of pepper, 40 pounds of flour or 14 pounds of margarine? It was necessary to divide everything into smaller portions. This meant a lot of lost time. It had also been discovered that the food would be much too heavy for the Dutch to digest. For too long they had been eating food that filled their bodies but which did not have any food value. A balanced diet was necessary in order to prevent people from eating themselves to death. Unfortunately people did kill themselves by gorging. Therefore it was decided that every meal had to consist of carbohydrates (potatoes, bread, flour), fat, albumen (meat, cheese, dried egg) and starch. Finally the means of distribution had to assure fair shares to everyone to prevent fights and discontent.

Nevertheless many people sighed: 'Now the food is there and yet we starve because we do not receive it. The effort to distribute as fairly as possible has caused delays and has caused deaths.'

During the third week of May a representative of the British Ministry of Food travelled through the Netherlands. His prime interest was the recently liberated West of the country. Deeply impressed he wrote a report a few days later:

'Communal Kitchens are providing more than 1,000 people with a small plate of soup daily. Children wandering through the street having no socks, no shoes. In the hospitals I saw babies looking like little old men. They gaze at you with big expressionless eyes. In the streets people watch with hungry faces when one eats a piece of chocolate without thinking. The lust has disappeared from their eyes. They are dressed in rags and seem to have lost all will to survive.'

In order to fight the problem of malnutrition, the British had a special preparation available consisting of albumen and carbohydrates. It could be eaten or be injected. It proved to be very unsuccessful with the Dutch. After a few days people started to refuse the very sweet substance. One of the reasons for the refusal must have been the strong desire to chew on a hearty and fragrant meal . . .

Until the moment when the first food stocks were distributed among the people around May 16th, the following figures shows a picture of cities: In Amsterdam approximately 30,000 suffered of malnutrition, in The Hague there were over 20,000. The situation was worse in Rotterdam: no less than 55,000 people suffered of oedema. On June 6th, one month after the Germans had laid down their arms the British Ambassador Sir Neville Bland investigated the area. In the May days of 1940, Sir Neville and his wife had to leave The Hague in a hurry; on May 25th 1945 he returned to his old post and visited his prewar friends. With his wife, he viewed the situation. 'The streets are empty and dirty, filth floats in the canals. Holland has lost its buoyany. It will be a long time before they are back at the level of 1939.'

In the month of May no less than 250,000 people had to be taken care of in hospitals. Almost 200,000 fellow-countrymen and women needed daily care at home. With this in mind one can call it a miracle that 'only' 20,000 people did not survive the Hunger Winter. The Allied food supplies could not have come much later.

After the final liberation of the Netherlands everyone was again able to say and think what he wanted. A strong urge to express the people's gratitude for the food aid given by the Allied air forces was felt. A news bulletin from the Air Ministry gives us an idea of the way the people showed their appreciation. We quote Air Ministry Bulletin number 19218. Above the bulletin an embargo has been printed. We do not know the reason for this, but we quote it also:

Not for publication, broadcast in overseas bulletins or use on club tapes before 2330
Double British Summer Time on Thursday, July 12, 1945 (i.e. for Friday
morningpapers). Not to be broadcast in the midnight news of 12th/13th July 1945.
Overseas messages should be prefaced with this embargo.
Dutch citizens' 'Thank you' to RAF.

The burghers of Voorburg, a large suburb of The Hague, have presented an illustrated testimonial, containing more than 5,000 signatures, to the RAF as a mark of gratitude for the airborne food supplies and as a tribute to the work of the RAF throughout the war. Air Vice-Marshal F.C. Huddleston, CB, CBE, the Air Officer Commanding 84 Group, RAF 2nd TAF, has accepted the gift on behalf of the RAF and has expressed the thanks of the service to the donors.

The presentation was organized by members of the Portico Club, which itself has an interesting history. Two Dutch journalists, Mr. and Mrs. Willink, installed a concealed radio in their home, powered by a dynamo driven by a bicycle, the Germans having cut off the electric supply. In the event of a German raid whilst Mr. and Mrs. Willink were taking a shorthand note of the BBC's news bulletin, the radio set could be hastily concealed in its secret cubby hole and Mr. Willink could disarm suspicion by starting to shave, thus explaining the presence of the dynamo. After the news each evening a number of friends would assemble at the Willinks' home and have it re-read to them by Mrs. Willink. In this way the Germans were tricked for four years.

Almost hysterical with joy at the sight of RAF Lancasters dropping the food parcels, the townsfolk at once decided to express their gratitude in some tangible form. Within six days the 130 page testimonial was finished. Prefacing the 5,000 signatures is a neat and colourful illustration of a Dutch town, symbolizing the tranquillity of Dutch suburban life. Under it are the words 'Voorburg, a suburb of The Hague, expresses its gratitude to the RAF for the airborne food supplies'. Following it are the signatures of the Mayor and Alderman of Voorburg, who, on behalf of the townsfolk, state: 'We thank you, British people, from the bottom of our hearts, for your willingness to send help to our small nation which you clearly demonstrated to us by the proud spectacle of your mighty air force soaring over our roofs carrying foodstuffs of which we stand in bitter need.' The testimonial also includes the signatures of the patients at the largest hospital in Voorburg, and also those of the Netherlands Interior Forces in the district. A moving ballad, eulogizing the 'Allied bombers that brought food to hungered Holland', written specially by Mr. Y. Foppema, a journalist on the staff of the *Haagsche Post* also appears in the work.

Throughout the testimonial appear the words, in red and blue, 'Thank you RAF' together with colourful sketches depicting the joy of the inhabitants at the food dropping and many stirring tributes to the air forces.

When a RAF party arrived at The Hague on the first day of the liberation it was met by a deputation from Voorburg made up of the chairman, secretary and other representatives of the Portico Club and two Dutch girls who had collected most of the signatures. The deputation formally handed over the testimonial for transmission to Air Vice-Marshal Huddleston, the RAF commander in the area. Acknowledging the gift Air Vice-Marshal Huddleston stated: 'We in the RAF have all had the greatest admiration for the magnificent stoicism developed by the people of Holland during the long days of German occupation and for their willing acceptance and understanding of those attacks it was necessary for us to make on enemy objectives in the Netherlands during that time. I am sending your gift to the AOC-in-C, 2nd TAF for onward transmission to the appropriate authority in England and permanent retention in the archives of the RAF. It will always remain one of our most treasured and valued possessions.'

Appendices

Appendix A
Daily reports of RAF and USAAF during the food drops

Report RAF Bomber Command 29th April 1945

Very bad weather conditions with heavy cloud were encountered for the first half of the route. Cloud base at 500-600 feet and rain and snow showers. The weather improved from 0300 degrees East, the base of the clouds lifting and the cloud tending to disperse. Near the Dutch coast there were only occasional patches of cloud with excellent visibility. Crews were able to map read to their respective dropping areas which could be visually identified. Although the green lights outlining the perimeter of the dropping zone and the white cross were clearly visible, the smoke from the red TI markers tended to obscure the white cross. The Dutch population had turned out in force to watch the operation and were reported to be waving to our crews as they passed over. All the bags are reported to have been dropped successfully, within the perimeter of the respective dropping areas. No opposition was encountered.

Report RAF Bomber Command 30th April 1945

Heavy rain showers were met at frequent intervals on the outward journey. Clouds down to 1,500 feet. Fortunately there were some good breaks over Holland and excellent visibility. The crews had no difficulty in map reading their way to their respective dropping areas. These were easily identified by the white cross and the TI's were seen overshooting the dropping areas as briefed. In spite of this overshooting there was some tendency owing to wind direction for the smoke to obscure the white cross. Dropping appeared to be very accurate with a very little scatter. As yesterday, crowds of Dutch people were out to watch the proceedings and waved enthusiastically to the crews.

Report RAF Bomber Command 1st May 1945

Clouds with base 1,000 to 1,500 feet were encountered en route to the dropping areas with occasional showers throughout the operation. The immediate vicinity of the dropping areas remained free from clouds during the dropping proceedings. Crews had no difficulties in identifying the dropping zones visually and were assisted in this by the smoke of the TI's. Many crews report that the white crosses were hardly visible due for the most part to the water logged state of the ground, particulary in the case of Aiming Point 4F (Kralingsche Plas). The dropping however was reasonably compact and confined to the dropping zone with the exception of a few bags which were seen to fall in the lake short of Aiming Point 4F. No opposition was encountered. Weather on the return journey was similar to that encountered on the outward journey.

Report Headquarters Eighth Air Force, 1st May 1945

4 b-17's and one p-51 as weather scouts for the bomber force engaged in supply dropping over Holland. Ten group formations sortied on food dropping mission in The Hague and Rotterdam areas. 392 a/c dropped 777.1 tons (34,534 containers) of ten-in-one rations on assigned targets at 0854-1050 hours from 320-800 feet. Weather 7/10-10/10 cloud above 1,000 feet over The Hague. Visibility 6-10 miles. Photographic intelligence indicates all boxes were dropped near the target areas and in generally good order. Some boxes falling in inundated areas. Crews of last squadron report civilians picking up food while it was still being dropped.

Report RAF Bomber Command 2nd May 1945

Low cloud and rain was encountered on most of the route and over the target, where cloud base was at 1,500-2,000 feet. It did not interfere with the operation. The dropping areas were easily identified, were correctly and plentifully marked. Dropping was accurate and concentrated. The dropping zone appeared very damp and several bags were apparently damaged by the obstructions on the ground which caused them to burst. The usual crowds were seen watching the proceedings and a large note was seen northwest of the dropping zone at Rotterdam, saying 'Many Thanks'. Weather improved slightly for the return journey.

Report Headquarters Eighth Air Force, 2nd May 1945

4 Mosquitoes completed weather reconnaissance over Holland, SE and Central Germany, North Sea and Atlantic S. of Ireland. 17 a/c (8b-17's and 9 p-51's as escort) dropped leaflets over France, Germany and Holland. 48 squadrons sortied on food dropping mission to Holland. 393 a/c dropped 767.1 tons (34,762 containers) of ten-in-one rations in assigned areas at 0921-1352 hours from 300-600 feet. Weather 4/10-6/10 cloud in Amsterdam area. Flak: one squadron encountered 20.mm fire along route which ceased immediately when green flare was fired. Battle damage: one major, three minor. Results: photos and personal accounts indicate that food dropping was successful with majority falling in populated areas. Late squadrons reported seeing civilians stacking up boxes.

Report RAF Bomber Command 3rd May 1945

Strato-cumulus with base varying from 1,000-3,000 feet persisted along the outward route. The dropping areas were covered with 10/10 clouds with base at 1,200 feet. Visibility below clouds was good and crews were able to identify the areas visually without difficulties. The smoke from the red TI's in all cases assisted crews in identification. The dropping was confined to the appointed areas and was in good concentration. No opposition was encountered.

Report Headquarters Eighth Air Force 3rd May 1945

Two Mosquitoes on special operation over Holland and Germany. One effective, losses nil. Ten group formations sortied on food dropping mission to Holland. 395 a/c dropped 739.1 tons in assigned areas at 0923-1145 hrs from 300-700 feet. Weather generally 5/10-8/10 clouds between 600-2,000 feet. Photographic intelligence indicates that all containers were dropped on or near target in generally good order.

RAF Bomber Command 4th May 1945
Over the North Sea cloud base was down to 1,000 feet and sometimes showers came down. The base of the cloud lifted somewhat as the aircraft reached the Dutch coast and visibility was good. No difficulty was experienced in identifying the dropping areas and all crews were able to map read their way to the respective dropping areas. The great majority of the bags are reported to have fallen within the prescribed areas. Crews report that in addition to the usual messages of thanks displayed in the fields and on the roof tops words as 'Tobacco Please' were noted, marked in a similar fashion. Weather on return was similar to the outward journey. No opposition of any kind was encountered.

Report Headquarters Eighth Air Force 4th May 1945
No USAAF food supply missions were flown on this day.

Report RAF Bomber Command 5th May 1945
We have not been able to trace the RAF Bomber Command report for this day.

Report Headquarters Eighth Air Force 5th May 1945
6 a/c (5 -B-17's and 1 P-51) as weather scouts for food dropping mission over Holland. 5 P-47's sortied effectively as airborne radio relays operating off Den Helder. Losses nil. 40 Squadrons sortied on food dropping mission to Holland. 402 a/c dropped 774.5 tons (84,119 British containers) of rations on assigned areas at 0918-1152 hours from 200-650 feet. Weather: 5/10-7/10 cloud over Holland with basis at 1,500 ft. Heavy rain shower encountered just after dropping on Amsterdam/Schiphol airfield. Visibility generally 3-6 miles. Flak: nil. One aircraft reported being fired on by 3 Germans using rifles at 1020 hours at 5236N/0440E (SW of Alkmaar airfield).

Report RAF Bomber Command 6th May 1945
Due to bad weather conditions no RAF drops were flown that day.

Report Headquarters Eighth Air Force 6th May 1945
4 a/c (3 B-17's and 1 P-51) as weather scouts for supply dropping missions. Ten groups sortied on food dropping mission over Holland. 381 a/c dropped 693.3 tons (78,105 British containers, 90 American containers) in assigned areas at 1304-1527 hours from 250-600 feet. Weather: 6/10-9/10 cloud, bases 1,500-2,800 feet. Visibility 8-12 miles.

Report RAF Bomber Command 7th May 1945
Patches of stratus clouds with tops at approx. 400-500 feet were found over England and crossing the North Sea. From the time, however, that our a/c crossed the Dutch coast the stratus had dispersed and visibility was excellent. No trouble was experienced in locating the dropping areas which were well marked by red TI's. The white cross was clearly visible and dropping was reported to have been accurate with the great majority of bags within the area. No opposition was encountered.

Report Eighth Air Force Headquarters 7th May 1945
10 B-24's on leaflet mission to France, Holland and the Channel Islands. 10 effective sorties. 1 B-17 airborne as radio relay. 1 B-17 on special mission over Holland. Six groups sortied on food dropping mission over Holland. 229 aircraft dropped 426 tons (48,137 British containers) in assigned areas at 1343-1508 hours from 200-800 feet. Visibility 4-7 miles. One a/c reported fired on by Germans using. 30 cal. rifle at 5227N/0438E. Battle damage 1 major. Losses: 1 B-17 ditched in North Sea.

Report RAF Bomber Command 8th May 1945
The entire route was covered by clouds with base at 2,000 feet and patches of sea fog were encountered. Otherwise visibility was good and crews had no difficulty in identifying the dropping areas visually. The white cross and the red light in area 1A was particulary distinct. The cross on area 4F however was not observed. The dropping in all areas was concentrated. No opposition was encountered.

Report Headquarters Eighth Air Force 8th May 1945
No food supply missions were flown that day.

Sometimes the bombers flew so low that the crews could read the time on the clock faces of church steeples. Here the clock of Ouderkerk shows 2:10 p.m.

Appendix B
The road to Manna and Chowhound: a chronology

17th September 1944: Operation Market Garden, railway strikes in Holland.

25th September 1944: German embargo on food transport from eastern Holland to the densely populated West.

26th September 1944: Last British airbornes withdraw from the Northern bank of the Rhine River.

5th October 1944: Dutch PM Gerbrandy urges Dutch railway workers to continue the strikes.

9th October 1944: Supply of electricity to civilians stops.

25th October 1944: Supply of gas to people of Amsterdam stops.

30th October 1944: First food supplies from Friesland reach Amsterdam via Zuiderzee/IJsselmeer.

10/11 November 1944: 50,000 men in Rotterdam arrested and sent to Germany.

4th December 1944: Bread rations cut down to 2 pounds a week.

6th December 1944: Germans remove electric trains and overhead lines to Germany.

14th December 1944: Total prohibition of electricity in North and South Holland provinces.

16th December 1944: German offensive into the Ardennes.

24th December 1944: Each Dutchman between 16 and 60 years of age has to report for forced labour. The 'Liese-Enterprises' cause mass arrests. Beginning of the first 'Famine-Tours' from the western part of the country to the agricultural East. Mass confiscations of obtained food by Germans and Dutch Nazis on return.

14th January 1945: HM Queen Wilhelmina appeals for help to HM King George VI and President Roosevelt.

15th January 1945: First regular distribution of sugar beets.

28th January 1945: Arrival in Delfzijl of two Swedish relief vessels.

24th February 1945: Dutch PM Gerbrandy asks for Allied offensive into western Holland.

27th February 1945: First distribution of Swedish food.

28th February 1945: Arrival of Swedish vessel Hallaren.

8th March 1945: Arrival of Portugese ship with food.

14th March 1945: Combined Chiefs of Staff order Eisenhower to prepare an offensive to liberate western Holland.

30th March 1945: Allied offensive across the Rhine to the north.

2nd April	1945:	German governor Seyss-Inquart says he is willing to negotiate food import.
12th April	1945:	President Roosevelt dies. Offensive into western Holland considered too costly and therefore abandoned.
14th April	1945:	Two representatives of the Dutch Resistance are allowed to cross the lines and contact the Allies.
15th April	1945:	PM Gerbrandy explains German proposals.
18th April	1945:	Entire east of the Netherlands except Delfzijl free.
21st April	1945:	Dutch Resistance objects to negotiations with Germans.
22nd April	1945:	Dutch government favours negotiations.
23rd April	1945:	Eisenhower gets permission to declare a temporary truce.
24th April	1945:	First radio message from London informs the Dutch in Occupied Territory about the coming drops.
25th April	1945:	Germans reject air drops.
26th April	1945:	First Manna-flight postponed due to bad weather.
28th April	1945:	Sir Francis De Guingand, Chief of Staff of Montgomery meets Dr. Schwebel, representative of Seyss-Inquart at the St. Joseph School in Achterveld.
29th April	1945:	OPERATION MANNA BEGINS
30 April	1945:	General Bedell Smith, Chief of Staff of Eisenhower, meets Seyss-Inquart, German governor in the Occupied Part of the Netherlands, at the St. Joseph School at Achterveld.
1st May	1945:	OPERATION CHOWHOUND BEGINS.
2nd May	1945:	OPERATION FAUST BEGINS. Arrival of first Allied ships carrying food at Rotterdam, escorted by German naval ships.
4th May	1945:	Montgomery accepts German surrender at Lüneburg.
5th May	1945:	General Blaskowitz accepts Allied document for the surrender of German troops. Queen Wilhelmina addresses her people.
6th May	1945:	Formal unconditional surrender of the German troops in Western Netherlands signed at Wageningen.
7th May	1945:	German surrender at Reims. END OF OPERATION CHOWHOUND
8th May	1945:	Second German surrender at Berlin. END OF OPERATION MANNA.

Appendix C

Operation Manna – the British squadrons

No. 1 Group	–	Bawtry Hall, Bawtry, Yorkshire		
Commanding Officer	–	**Air Vice-Marshal R.S. Blucke**		
No. 12 Squadron: PA	–	RAF Wickenby, Lincs.	–	Lancasters
No. 100 Squadron: HW	–	RAF Elsham Wolds, Lincs.	–	Lancasters
No. 101 Squadron: SR	–	RAF Ludford Magna, Lincs.	–	Lancasters
No. 103 Squadron: PM	–	RAF Elsham Wolds, Lincs.	–	Lancasters
No. 150 Squadron: IQ	–	RAF Hemswell, Lincs.	–	Lancasters
No. 153 Squadron: P4	–	RAF Scampton, Lincs.	–	Lancasters
No. 166 Squadron: AS	–	RAF Kirmington, Lincs.	–	Lancasters
No. 170 Squadron: TC	–	RAF Hemswell, Lincs.	–	Lancasters
No. 300 Squadron: BH	–	RAF Faldingworth, Lincs. [1]	–	Lancasters
No. 460 Squadron: AR	–	RAF Binbrook, Lincs. [2]	–	Lancasters
No. 550 Squadron: BQ	–	RAF North Killingholme, Lincs.	–	Lancasters
No. 576 Squadron: UL	–	RAF Fiskerton, Lincs.	–	Lancasters
No. 625 Squadron: CF	–	RAF Scampton, Lincs.	–	Lancasters
No. 626 Squadron: UM	–	RAF Wickenby, Lincs.	–	Lancasters

No. 3 Group	–	Exning, Suffolk		
Commanding Officer	–	**Air Vice-Marshal R. Harrison**		
No. 15 Squadron: LS	–	RAF Mildenhall, Suffolk	–	Lancasters
No. 75 Squadron: AA, JN	–	RAF Mepal, Cambs. [3]	–	Lancasters
No. 90 Squadron: WP	–	RAF Tuddenham, Suffolk	–	Lancasters
No. 115 Squadron: KO, A4, IL	–	RAF Witchford, Cambs.	–	Lancasters
No. 138 Squadron: AC, NF	–	RAF Tuddenham, Suffolk	–	Lancasters
No. 149 Squadron: OJ	–	RAF Methwold, Suffolk	–	Lancasters
No. 186 Squadron: XY, AP	–	RAF Stradishall, Suffolk	–	Lancasters
No. 195 Squadron: A4, JE	–	RAF Wratting Common, Cambs.	–	Lancasters
No. 218 Squadron: HA	–	RAF Chedburgh, Suffolk	–	Lancasters
No. 514 Squadron: J1, A2	–	RAF Waterbeach, Lincs.	–	Lancasters
No. 622 Squadron: CF	–	RAF Mildenhall, Suffolk	–	Lancasters

No. 8 Group PFF	–	Castle Hill House, Hunts.		
Commanding Officer	–	**Air Vice-Marshall D.C.T. Bennett**		
No. 7 Squadron: MG	–	RAF Oakington, Cambs.	–	Lancasters
No. 35 Squadron: TL	–	RAF Graveley, Hunts.	–	Lancasters
No. 105 Squadron: GB	–	RAF Bourn, Cambs.	–	Mosquito's
No. 109 Squadron: HS	–	RAF Little Staughton, Hunts.	–	Mosquito's
No. 156 Squadron: GT	–	RAF Upwood, Hunts.	–	Lancasters
No. 405 Squadron: LQ	–	RAF Gransden Lodge, Beds. [4]	–	Lancasters
No. 582 Squadron: 60	–	RAF Little Staughton, Hunts.	–	Lancasters
No. 635 Squadron: F2	–	RAF Downham Market, Norfolk	–	Lancasters

[1] No. 300 (Polish) Squadron.
[2] No. 460 (RAAF) Squadron.
[3] No. 75 (RNZAF) Squadron.
[4] No. 405 (RCAF) Squadron.

Appendix D

Operation Chowhound – the American Bomb Groups

13 Combat Wing
95th Bombardment Group (H)   –   334th, 335th, 336th, 412th BS [1])
                                    Horham, B17G Flying Fortress
Commanding Officer   –   Lieutenant-Colonel R.H. Stuart
100th Bombardment Group (H)   –   349th, 350th, 351st, 418th BS
                                    Thorpe Abbots, B17G
Commanding Officer   –   Lieutenant-Colonel J.M. Bennett Jr.
390th Bombardment Group (H)   –   568th, 569th, 570th BS
                                    Framlingham, B17G
Commanding Officer   –   Colonel Joseph A. Moller

45 Combat Wing
96th Bombardment Group (H)   –   337th, 338th, 339th BS
                                    Snetterton Heath, B17G
Commanding Officer   –   Colonel Robert W. Warren
388th Bombardment Group (H)   –   560th, 561st, 562nd, 563rd BS
                                    Knettishall, B17G
Commanding Officer   –   Colonel Chester C. Cos
452nd Bombardment Group (H)   –   728th, 729th, 730th, 731st BS
                                    Deopham Green, B17G
Commanding Officer   –   Colonel Burnham L. Batson

93 Combat Wing
34th Bombardment Group (H)   –   4th, 8th, 18th, 391st BS
                                    Mendlesham, B17G
Commanding Officer   –   Colonel William E. Creer
385th Bombardment Group (H)   –   548th, 549th, 550th, 551st BS
                                    Great Ashfield
Commanding Officer   –   Colonel George Y. Jumper
490th Bombardment Group (H)   –   848th, 849th, 851st BS
                                    Eye, B17G
Commanding Officer   –   Colonel Frank P. Bostrom
493th Bombardment Group (H)   –   860st, 861st, 862nd, 863rd BS
                                    Debach, B17G
Commanding Officer   –   Colonel Robert B. Landry

[1]) BS: Bombardment Squadron.

Squadron codes Nos. 1, 3, 8 (PFF) Group, Bomber Command RAF:

NO. 1 GROUP:	NO. 3 GROUP:	NO. 8 GROUP (PFF):
No. 12 Squadron: PH	No. 15 Squadron: LS	No. 7 Squadron: MG
No. 100 Squadron: HW	No. 75 Squadron: AA, JN	No. 35 Squadron: TL
No. 101 Squadron: SR	No. 90 Squadron: WP	No. 105 Squadron: GB
No. 103 Squadron: PM	No. 115 Squadron: KO, A4, IL	No. 109 Squadron: HS
No. 150 Squadron: IQ	No. 138 Squadron: AC, NF	No. 156 Squadron: GT
No. 153 Squadron: P4	No. 149 Squadron: OJ	No. 405 Squadron: LQ
No. 166 Squadron: AS	No. 186 Squadron: XY, AP	No. 582 Squadron: 60
No. 170 Squadron: TC	No. 195 Squadron: A4, JE	No. 635 Squadron: F2
No. 300 Squadron: BH	No. 218 Squadron: HA	
No. 460 Squadron: AR	No. 514 Squadron: J1, A2	
No. 550 Squadron: BQ	No. 622 Squadron: GI	
No. 576 Squadron: UL		
No. 625 Squadron: CF		
No. 626 Squadron: UM		

Group and Squadron codes 3rd Air Divison, USAAF:

13 Combat Wing:

95th Bombardment Group : Ⓑ	334th Bombardment Squadron: BG
	335th Bombardment Squadron: OE
	336th Bombardment Squadron: ET
	412th Bombardment Squadron: QW

100th Bombardment Group : Ⓓ	349th Bombardment Squadron: XR
	350th Bombardment Squadron: LN
	351st Bombardment Squadron: EP
	418th Bombardment Squadron: LD

390th Bombardment Group : Ⓙ	568th Bombardment Squadron: BI
	569th Bombardment Squadron: CC
	570th Bombardment Squadron: DI
	571st Bombardment Squadron: FC

45 Combat Wing:

96th Bombardment Group : Ⓒ	337th Bombardment Squadron: QJ
	338th Bombardment Squadron: BX
	339th Bombardment Squadron: AW
	413th Bombardment Squadron: MZ

388th Bombardment Group : Ⓗ	560th Bombardment Squadron: –
	561st Bombardment Squadron: –
	562nd Bombardment Squadron: –
	563rd Bombardment Squadron: –

452nd Bombardment Group : Ⓛ	728th Bombardment Squadron: 9Z
	729th Bombardment Squadron: M3
	730th Bombardment Squadron: 6K
	731st Bombardment Squadron: 7D

93 Combat Wing:

34th Bombardment Group : S	4th Bombardment Squadron: Q6
	7th Bombardment Squadron: R2
	18th Bombardment Squadron: 81
	391st Bombardment Squadron: 3L

385th Bombardment Group : G	548th Bombardment Squadron: GX
	549th Bombardment Squadron: XA
	550th Bombardment Squadron: SG
	551st Bombardment Squadron: HR

490th Bombardment Group : T	848th Bombardment Squadron: 7W
	849th Bombardment Squadron: W8
	850th Bombardment Squadron: 7Q
	851st Bombardment Squadron: S3

493rd Bombardment Group : X	860th Bombardment Squadron: NG
	861st Bombardment Squadron: Q4
	862nd Bombardment Squadron: 8M
	863rd Bombardment Squadron: G8

Appendix E
Schedule of droppings

29 April 1945:   RAF

Valkenburg	No. 8 Group	4 Mosquitoes	(4)	Pathfinders	
	No. 1 Group	59 Lancasters	(57)	119.3 tons	
Duindigt	No. 8 Group	4 Mosquitoes	(3)	Pathfinders	
	No. 1 Group	57 Lancasters	(57)	122.6 tons	
Ypenburg	No. 8 Group	4 Mosquitoes	(3)	Pathfinders	
	No. 1 Group	32 Lancasters	(31)	70.7 tons	
	No. 3 Group	31 Lancasters	(31)	70.0 tons	
Waalhaven	No. 8 Group	4 Mosquitoes	(4)	Pathfinders	
	No. 3 Group	63 Lancasters	(59)	134.9 tons	
Haamstede[1])	No. 3 Group	– Lancasters	(4)	9.0 tons	
Meteo recce	No. 8 Group	2 Mosquitoes	(2)		
	No. 8 Group	18 Mosquitoes	(16)		
	No. 1 Group	148 Lancasters	(145)	312.6 tons	
	No. 3 Group	94 Lancasters	(94)	213.9 tons	
		242 Lancasters	(239)	. 526.5 tons	

[1]) target of opportunity.

30 April 1945:   RAF

Valkenburg	No. 8 Group	4 Mosquitoes	(4)	Pathfinders	
	No. 8 Group	5 Lancasters	(5)	10.5 tons PFF	
	No. 1 Group	90 Lancasters	(90)	175.8 tons	
Duindigt	No. 8 Group	4 Mosquitoes	(4)	Pathfinders	
	No. 8 Group	5 Lancasters	(5)	10.5 tons PFF	
	No. 1 Group	90 Lancasters	(90)	195.4 tons	
Ypenburg	No. 8 Group	4 Mosquitoes	(4)	Pathfinders	
	No. 8 Group	5 Lancasters	(5)	10.5 tons PFF	
	No. 1 Group	90 Lancasters	(89)	175.8 tons	
Terbregge	No. 8 Group	4 Mosquitoes	(3)	Pathfinders	
	No. 8 Group	11 Lancasters	(11)	23.1 tons PFF	
	No. 3 Group	188 Lancasters	(187)	403.7 tons	
Meteo recce	No. 8 Group	4 Mosquitoes	(4)		
	No. 8 Group	20 Mosquitoes	(19)		
	No. 8 Group	26 Lancasters	(26)	54.6 tons PFF	
	No. 1 Group	270 Lancasters	(269)	547.0 tons	
	No. 3 Group	188 Lancasters	(187)	403.7 tons	
		484 Lancasters	(482)	1005.3 tons	

Mosquitoes and Lancasters of No. 8 (PFF) Group made sure the Lancasters of Nos. 1 and 3 Group could find their targets. They marked the drop zones with red markers. Their airfields were situated between Cambridge and Peterborough.

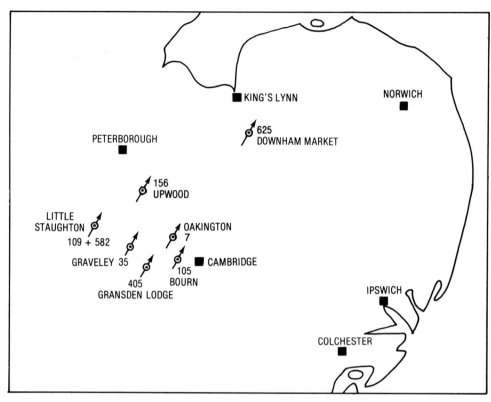

The airfields of the Chowhound-crews were situated between Norwich and Ipswich.

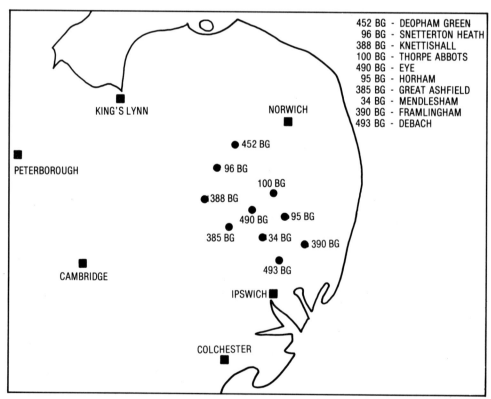

1 May 1945	RAF			
Valkenburg	No. 8 Group	4 Mosquitoes	(3)	Pathfinders
	No. 1 Group	46 Lancasters	(46)	103.0 tons
Duindigt	No. 8 Group	4 Mosquitoes	(4)	Pathfinders
	No. 8 Group	6 Lancasters	(6)	12.6 tons PFF
	No. 3 Group	93 Lancasters	(93)	212.8 tons
Ypenburg	No. 8 Group	4 Mosquitoes	(4)	Pathfinders
	No. 8 Group	6 Lancasters	(6)	12.6 tons
	No. 3 Group	98 Lancasters	(98)	227.4 tons
Terbregge	No. 8 Group	4 Mosquitoes	(4)	Pathfinders
	No. 8 Group	16 Lancasters	(12)	25.2 tons PFF
	No. 1 Group	277 Lancasters	(227)	502.3 tons
Meteo recce	No. 8 Group	2 Mosquitoes	(2)	
	No. 8 Group	18 Mosquitoes	(17)	
	No. 8 Group	28 Lancasters	(24)	50.4 tons PFF
	No. 1 Group	273 Lancasters	(273)	605.3 tons
	No. 3 Group	191 Lancasters	(191)	440.2 tons
		492 Lancasters	(488)	1095.9 tons

1 May 1945	USAAF			
Valkenburg	390 BG(H)	40 B-17G	(40)	77.6 tons
	100 BG(H)	40 B-17G	(37)	71.7 tons
Duindigt	95 BG(H)	40 B-17G	(40)	77.5 tons
	452 BG(H)	40 B-17G	(39)	75.6 tons
Ypenburg	96 BG(H)	40 B-17G	(40)	79.5 tons
	388 BG(H)	41 B-17G	(41)	81.5 tons
Terbregge	34 BG(H)	36 B-17G	(36)	72.9 tons
	385 BG(H)	41 B-17G	(41)	82.5 tons
	490 BG(H)	40 B-17G	(40)	81.0 tons
	493 BG(H)	38 B-17G	(38)	76.3 tons
3rd Air Division		396 B-17G	(392)	776.1 tons

2 May 1945	RAF			
Valkenburg	No. 8 Group	4 Mosquitoes	(3)	Pathfinders
	No. 1 Group	42 Lancasters	(42)	93.5 tons
Duindigt	No. 8 Group	4 Mosquitoes	(4)	Pathfinders
	No. 8 Group	5 Lancasters	(5)	10.5 tons PFF
	No. 3 Group	94 Lancasters	(91)	206.6 tons
Ypenburg	No. 8 Group	4 Mosquitoes	(4)	Pathfinders
	No. 8 Group	5 Lancasters	(5)	10.5 tons
	No. 3 Group	97 Lancasters	(97)	224.0 tons
Terbregge	No. 8 Group	4 Mosquitoes	(2)	Pathfinders
	No. 8 Group	16 Lancasters	(15)	31.5 tons
	No. 1 Group	216 Lancasters	(216)	478.3 tons
Gouda	No. 8 Group	4 Mosquitoes	(3)	Pathfinders
	No. 1 Group	12 Lancasters	(12)	26.7 tons
Meteo recce	No. 8 Group	1 Mosquitoe	(1)	
	No. 8 Group	21 Mosquitoes	(16)	
	No. 8 Group	26 Lancasters	(25)	52.5 tons PFF
	No. 1 Group	228 Lancasters	(228)	505.0 tons
	No. 3 Group	233 Lancasters	(230)	524.1 tons
		487 Lancasters	(483)	1081.6 tons

2 May 1945 — USAAF

Schiphol	95 BG(H)	40 B-17G	(38)	74.7 tons
	96 BG(H)	38 B-17G	(37)	72.8 tons
	100 BG(H)	40 B-17G	(39)	72.8 tons
	388 BG(H)	40 B-17G	(39)	76.7 tons
	390 BG(H)	40 B-17G	(38)	74.7 tons
	452 BG(H)	40 B-17G	(40)	78.7 tons
	490 BG(H)	20 B-17G	(19)	37.4 tons
Vogelenzang	493 BG(H)	40 B-17G	(40)	79.0 tons
Bergen	490 BG(H)	7 B-17G	(7)	11.7 tons
	452 BG(H)	14 B-17G	(13)	21.8 tons
Hilversum	385 BG(H)	20 B-17G	(20)	40.5 tons
Utrecht	34 BG(H)	40 B-17G	(38)	74.3 tons
	385 BG(H)	22 B-17G	(21)	41.1 tons
North-Alkmaar			(1)	1.9 tons
NW-Edam			(1)	1.9 tons
South-Weesp			(1)	1.9 tons
North-Leerdam			(1)	1.3 tons
3rd Air Division		401 B-17G	(393)	767.1 tons

2 May: four B-17G's of 385 BG(H) reported that German soldiers near Hilversum opened fire. This ceased after the Americans fired green flares. Three aircraft sustained minor damage, one aircraft received severe damage.

3 May 1945 — RAF

Valkenburg	No. 8 Group	4 Mosquitoes	(4)	Pathfinders
	No. 1 Group	22 Lancasters	(22)	48.7 tons
Duindigt	No. 8 Group	4 Mosquitoes	(4)	Pathfinders
	No. 8 Group	3 Lancasters	(3)	6.3 tons PFF
	No. 3 Group	54 Lancasters	(54)	137.2 tons
Ypenburg	No. 8 Group	4 Mosquitoes	(4)	Pathfinders
	No. 8 Group	3 Lancasters	(3)	6.3 tons PFF
	No. 3 Group	55 Lancasters	(55)	132.2 tons
Terbregge	No. 8 Group	4 Mosquitoes	(4)	Pathfinders
	No. 8 Group	14 Lancasters	(14)	29.4 tons PFF
	No. 1 Group	222 Lancasters	(222)	487.7 tons
Gouda	No. 8 Group	4 Mosquitoes	(4)	Pathfinders
	No. 1 Group	10 Lancasters	(10)	21.8 tons
Meteo recce	No. 8 Group	2 Mosquitoes	(2)	
	No. 8 Group	22 Mosquitoes	(22)	
	No. 8 Group	20 Lancasters	(20)	42.0 tons
	No. 1 Group	254 Lancasters	(254)	558.3 tons
	No. 3 Group	109 Lancasters	(109)	269.4 tons
		383 Lancasters	(383)	869.7 tons

3 May 1945   USAAF

Schiphol	34 BG(H)	39 B-17G	(34)	64.0 tons
	96 BG(H)	38 B-17G	(38)	71.5 tons
	385 BG(H)	34 B-17G	(34)	64.0 tons
	388 BG(H)	39 B-17G	(39)	73.4 tons
	452 BG(H)	38 B-17G	(38)	71.5 tons
	490 BG(H)	35 B-17G	(35)	65.9 tons
	493 BG(H)	33 B-17G	(33)	62.2 tons
Vogelenzang	34 BG(H)	5 B-17G	(5)	9.1 tons
	385 BG(H)	5 B-17G	(5)	9.1 tons
	490 BG(H)	5 B-17G	(5)	9.1 tons
	390 BG(H)	21 B-17G	(21)	38.3 tons
	493 BG(H)	6 B-17G	(6)	11.1 tons
Bergen	100 BG(H)	20 B-17G	(20)	37.7 tons
Hilversum	100 BG(H)	21 B-17G	(21)	37.7 tons
Utrecht	95 BG(H)	40 B-17G	(38)	72.5 tons
	390 BG(H)	20 B-17G	(20)	36.3 tons
Purmerend			(2)	3.8 tons
Haamstede			(1)	1.9 tons
3rd Air Division		399 B-17G	(395)	739.1 tons

4 May 1945   RAF

Valkenburg	No. 8 Group	4 Mosquitoes	(4)	Pathfinders
	No. 1 Group	11 Lancasters	(11)	24.6 tons
Duindigt	No. 8 Group	4 Mosquitoes	(4)	Pathfinders
	No. 8 Group	3 Lancasters	(1)	2.1 tons PFF
	No. 3 Group	28 Lancasters	(28)	73.4 tons
Ypenburg	No. 8 Group	4 Mosquitoes	(4)	Pathfinders
	No. 8 Group	3 Lancasters	(3)	6.3 tons PFF
	No. 3 Group	31 Lancasters	(30)	65.0 tons
Terbregge	No. 8 Group	4 Mosquitoes	(4)	Pathfinders
	No. 8 Group	14 Lancasters	(14)	29.4 tons PFF
	No. 1 Group	109 Lancasters	(108)	238.1 tons
Gouda	No. 8 Group	4 Mosquitoes	(4)	Pathfinders
	No. 1 Group	5 Lancasters	(5)	11.0 tons
Meteo recce	No. 8 Group	3 Mosquitoes	(3)	
	No. 8 Group	23 Mosquitoes	(23)	
	No. 8 Group	20 Lancasters	(18)	37.8 tons PFF
	No. 1 Group	125 Lancasters	(124)	273.7 tons
	No. 3 Group	59 Lancasters	(58)	138.4 tons
		204 Lancasters	(200)	449.9 tons

No drops USAAF

The food was dropped by Lancasters bombers of Nos. 1 and 3 Group. The airfields of No. 1 Group were situated between the Humber-river and the city of Lincoln; the airfields of No. 3 Group between Peterborough, Norwich, Ipswich and Cambridge.

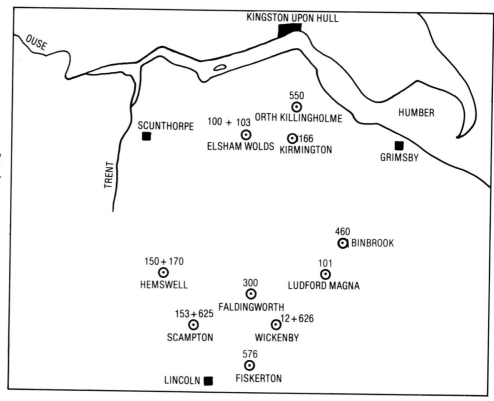

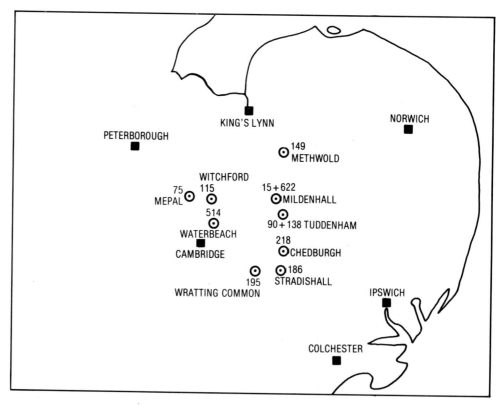

5 May 1945   RAF

Valkenburg	No. 8 Group	4 Mosquitoes	(4)	Pathfinders
	No. 1 Group	10 Lancasters	(10)	22.4 tons
Duindigt	No. 8 Group	4 Mosquitoes	(4)	Pathfinders
	No. 8 Group	3 Lancasters	(3)	6.3 tons PFF
	No. 3 Group	29 Lancasters	(28)	69.4 tons
Ypenburg	No. 8 Group	4 Mosquitoes	(4)	Pathfinders
	No. 8 Group	3 Lancasters	(3)	6.3 tons PFF
	No. 3 Group	27 Lancasters	(27)	60.3 tons
Terbregge	No. 8 Group	4 Mosquitoes	(3)	Pathfinders
	No. 8 Group	14 Lancasters	(11)	23.1 tons PFF
	No. 1 Group	108 Lancasters	(106)	234.6 tons
Gouda	No. 8 Group	4 Mosquitoes	(4)	Pathfinders
	No. 1 Group	5 Lancasters	(5)	11.2 tons
Meteo recce	No. 8 Group	1 Mosquitoe	(1)	
	No. 8 Group	21 Mosquitoes	(20)	
	No. 8 Group	20 Lancasters	(17)	35.7 tons
	No. 1 Group	123 Lancasters	(121)	268.2 tons
	No. 3 Group	56 Lancasters	(55)	129.7 tons
		199 Lancasters	(193)	433.6 tons

5 May 1945   USAAF

Schiphol	34 BG(H)	35 B-17G	(35)	64.4 tons
	96 BG(H)	40 B-17G	(40)	73.7 tons
	385 BG(H)	35 B-17G	(35)	64.4 tons
	388 BG(H)	40 B-17G	(40)	73.7 tons
	452 BG(H)	40 B-17G	(40)	73.7 tons
	490 BG(H)	36 B-17G	(36)	66.3 tons
	493 BG(H)	36 B-17G	(35)	64.4 tons
Vogelenzang	34 BG(H)	5 B-17G	(5)	9.4 tons
	385 BG(H)	5 B-17G	(5)	9.4 tons
	390 BG(H)	20 B-17G	(20)	37.7 tons
	490 BG(H)	5 B-17G	(5)	9.4 tons
	493 BG(H)	5 B-17G	(5)	9.5 tons
Bergen	100 BG(H)	21 B-17G	(21)	37.7 tons
Baarn[1])	100 BG(H)		(4)	7.4 tons
Hilversum	100 BG(H)	20 B-17G	(16)	30.2 tons
Utrecht	95 BG(H)	40 B-17G	(40)	75.4 tons
	390 BG(H)	20 B-17G	(20)	37.7 tons
3rd Air Division		403 B-17G	(402)	744.4 tons

5 May: a B-17G of 100 BG(H) reported German soldiers firing at aircraft from Bergen Airfield. This rifle fire caused only slight damage.

[1]) Target of opportunity.

6 May 1945:   USAAF

Schiphol	34 BG(H)	36 B-17G	(36)	66.5 tons
	96 BG(H)	35 B-17G	(35)	64.6 tons
	385 BG(H)	34 B-17G	(33)	61.0 tons
	388 BG(H)	36 B-17G	(36)	66.5 tons
	490 BG(H)	36 B-17G	(36)	66.5 tons
	452 BG(H)	36 B-17G	(35)	64.6 tons
	493 BG(H)	35 B-17G	(35)	64.6 tons
Vogelenzang	34 BG(H)	5 B-17G	(5)	9.5 tons
	385 BG(H)	6 B-17G	(6)	11.6 tons
	390 BG(H)	17 B-17G	(17)	32.9 tons
	490 BG(H)	4 B-17G	(4)	8.1 tons
	493 BG(H)	5 B-17G	(5)	9.6 tons
Bergen	100 BG(H)	18 B-17G	(18)	33.9 tons
Hilversum	100 BG(H)	19 B-17G	(18)	32.1 tons
Utrecht	95 BG(H)	39 B-17G	(39)	73.5 tons
	390 BG(H)	20 B-17G	(20)	37.6 tons

3rd Air Division	380 B-17G	(378)	703.1 tons

No drops RAF

7 May 1945:   RAF

Valkenburg	No. 8 Group	4 Mosquitoes	(4)	Pathfinders
	No. 8 Group	3 Lancasters	(3)	6.3 tons PFF
	No. 1 Group	51 Lancasters	(51)	118.4 tons
Duindigt	No. 8 Group	4 Mosquitoes	(4)	Pathfinders
	No. 8 Group	4 Lancasters	(4)	8.4 tons PFF
	No. 3 Group	71 Lancasters	(70)	174.6 tons
Ypenburg	No. 8 Group	4 Mosquitoes	(4)	Pathfinders
	No. 8 Group	4 Lancasters	(4)	8.4 tons PFF
	No. 3 Group	72 Lancasters	(72)	174.6 tons
Terbregge	No. 8 Group	4 Mosquitoes	(3)	Pathfinders
	No. 8 Group	16 Lancasters	(16)	33.6 tons PFF
	No. 1 Group	300 Lancasters	(299)	663.0 tons
Gouda	No. 8 Group	4 Mosquitoes	(3)	Pathfinders
	No. 3 Group	24 Lancasters	(24)	54.6 tons
Meteo recce	No. 8 Group	1 Mosquito	(1)	
	No. 8 Group	21 Mosquitoes	(19)	
	No. 8 Group	27 Lancasters	(27)	56.7 tons PFF
	No. 1 Group	351 Lancasters	(350)	781.4 tons
	No. 3 Group	167 Lancasters	(166)	384.8 tons

	545 Lancasters	(543)	1222.9 tons

7 May 1945 | | USAAF

Schiphol	34 BG(H)	39 B-17G	(39)	72.3 tons
	100 BG(H)	38 B-17G	(36)	66.8 tons
	385 BG(H)	39 B-17G	(39)	72.3 tons
	493 BG(H)	40 B-17G	(40)	74.2 tons
Vogelenzang	390 BG(H)	25 B-17G	(25)	46.2 tons
Bergen	390 BG(H)	10 B-17G	(10)	18.8 tons
Hilversum	95 BG(H)	12 B-17G	(12)	22.6 tons
Utrecht	95 BG(H)	28 B-17G	(28)	52.8 tons
		231 B-17G	(229)	426.0 tons

Over IJmuiden two B-17's (95 BG(H) and 385 BG(H)) were fired upon by German machine guns. The 95 BG(H) B-17G crashed into the North Sea. Of the crew of twelve only two survived.

8 May 1945 | | RAF

Duindigt	No. 8 Group	4 Mosquitoes	(4)	Pathfinders
	No. 8 Group	3 Lancasters	(3)	6.3 tons PFF
	No. 1 Group	44 Lancasters	(44)	97.6 tons
Ypenburg	No. 8 Group	4 Mosquitoes	(4)	Pathfinders
	No. 8 Group	3 Lancasters	(3)	6.3 tons PFF
	No. 3 Group	46 Lancasters	(46)	118.7 tons
Terbregge	No. 8 Group	4 Mosquitoes	(4)	Pathfinders
	No. 8 Group	3 Lancasters	(2)	4.2 tons PFF
	No. 1 Group	14 Lancasters	(13)	29.1 tons
	No. 3 Group	32 Lancasters	(32)	82.3 tons
Meteo recce	No. 8 Group	1 Mosquito	(1)	
	No. 8 Group	13 Mosquitoes	(13)	
	No. 8 Group	9 Lancasters	(8)	16.8 tons PFF
	No. 1 Group	58 Lancasters	(57)	126.7 tons
	No. 3 Group	78 Lancasters	(78)	201.0 tons
		145 Lancasters	(143)	344.5 tons

Total weights dropped by the RAF and USAAF during Manna/Chowhound:

	RAF	USAAF
29 April	556.5 tons	
30 April	1005.3 tons	
1 May	1095.9 tons	776.1 tons
2 May	1081.6 tons	767.1 tons
3 May	869.7 tons	739.1 tons
4 May	449.9 tons	–
5 May	433.6 tons	744.4 tons
6 May	–	703.1 tons
7 May	1222.9 tons	426.0 tons
8 May	344.5 tons	–
	7029.9 tons[1])	4155.8 tons[2])

[1]) RAF: 1 (long) ton: 2240 lb.

[2]) USAAF: 1 (short) ton: 2000 lb.

Number of aircraft detailed and (dropping) during Manna/Chowhound:

	RAF	USAAF	total number
29 April	242 (239)	–	242 (239)
30 April	484 (482)	–	484 (482)
1 May	492 (488)	396 (392)	888 (880)
2 May	487 (483)	401 (393)	888 (876)
3 May	383 (383)	399 (395)	782 (778)
4 May	204 (200)	– (–)	204 (200)
5 May	199 (193)	403 (402)	602 (595)
6 May	– (–)	380 (378)	380 (378)
7 May	545 (543)	231 (229)	776 (772)
8 May	145 (143)	– (–)	145 (143)
	3181 (3154) Lancasters	2210 (2189) B-17G's	5391 (5343)

total amount of aircraf detailed (effective) during Manna/Chowhound:

RAF	USAAF	total number
3181 (3154)	2210 (2189)	5391 (5343)
177 (165)	58 (46)	235 (211)
3358 (3319)	2268 (2235)	5626 (5554)

OPERATION MANNA-CHOWHOUND

RAF

USAAF

Number of aircraft detailed and (effective) for Marking, Weather Recce and Communications only during Manna/Chowhound.

	RAF	USAAF	total number
29 April	18 (16)	–	18 (16)
30 April	20 (19)	–	20 (19)
1 May	18 (17)	6 (6)	24 (23)
2 May	21 (16)	18 (18)	39 (34)
3 May	22 (22)	5 (4)	27 (26)
4 May	23 (23)	– (–)	23 (23)
5 May	21 (20)	11 (10)	32 (30)
6 May	– (–)	4 (4)	4 (4)
7 May	21 (19)	14 (14)	35 (33)
8 May	13 (13)	– (–)	13 (13)
	177 (165)	58 (46)	235 (211)

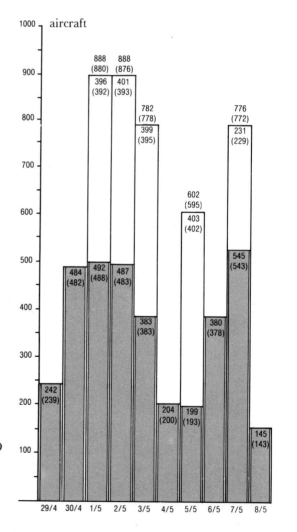

Tons of food dropped per day/per drop zone:

		RAF	USAAF				RAF	USAAF
Waalhaven	29 April	134.9 tons			Gouda	2 May	26.7 tons	
Terbregge	30 April	426.8 tons			Gouda	3 May	21.8 tons	
Terbregge	1 May	527.5 tons	312.7 tons		Gouda	4 May	11.0 tons	
Terbregge	2 May	509.8 tons			Gouda	5 May	11.2 tons	
Terbregge	3 May	517.2 tons			Gouda	6 May	–	
Terbregge	4 May	267.5 tons			Gouda	7 May	54.6 tons	
Terbregge	5 May	257.7 tons						
Terbregge	6 May	–					125.3 tons	
Terbregge	7 May	-696.6 tons			Schiphol	2 May		491.7 tons
Terbregge	8 May	115.6 tons			Schiphol	3 May		472.5 tons
					Schiphol	4 May		–
		3453.6 tons	312.7 tons		Schiphol	5 May		480.6 tons
					Schiphol	6 May		454.3 tons
Valkenburg	29 April	119.3 tons			Schiphol	7 May		285.6 tons
Valkenburg	30 April	186.3 tons						
Valkenburg	1 May	103.0 tons	149.3 tons					2184.7 tons
Valkenburg	2 May	93.5 tons						
Valkenburg	3 May	48.7 tons			Vogelenzang	2 May		79.0 tons
Valkenburg	4 May	24.6 tons			Vogelenzang	3 May		76.7 tons
Valkenburg	5 May	22.4 tons			Vogelenzang	4 May		–
Valkenburg	6 May	–			Vogelenzang	5 May		75.4 tons
Valkenburg	7 May	124.7 tons			Vogelenzang	6 May		71.7 tons
Valkenburg	8 May	–			Vogelenzang	7 May		46.2 tons
		722.5 tons	149.3 tons					349.0 tons
Duindigt	29 April	122.6 tons			Bergen	2 May		33.5 tons
Duindigt	30 April	205.9 tons			Bergen	3 May		37.7 tons
Duindigt	1 May	225.4 tons	153.1 tons		Bergen	4 May		–
Duindigt	2 May	217.1 tons			Bergen	5 May		37.7 tons
Duindigt	3 May	143.5 tons			Bergen	6 May		33.9 tons
Duindigt	4 May	75.5 tons			Bergen	7 May		18.8 tons
Duindigt	5 May	75.7 tons						
Duindigt	6 May	–						161.6 tons
Duindigt	7 May	164.0 tons						
Duindigt	8 May	103.9 tons			Hilversum	2 May		40.5 tons
					Hilversum	3 May		37.7 tons
		1333.6 tons	153.1 tons		Hilversum	4 May		–
					Hilversum	5 May		30.2 tons
Ypenburg	29 April	140.7 tons			Hilversum	6 May		32.1 tons
Ypenburg	30 April	186.3 tons			Hilversum	7 May		22.6 tons
Ypenburg	1 May	240.0 tons	161.0 tons					
Ypenburg	2 May	234.5 tons						163.1 tons
Ypenburg	3 May	138.5 tons						
Ypenburg	4 May	71.3 tons			Utrecht	2 May		115.4 tons
Ypenburg	5 May	66.6 tons			Utrecht	3 May		108.8 tons
Ypenburg	6 May	–			Utrecht	4 May		–
Ypenburg	7 May	183.0 tons			Utrecht	5 May		113.1 tons
Ypenburg	8 May	125.0 tons			Utrecht	6 May		111.1 tons
					Utrecht	7 May		52.8 tons
		1385.9 tons	161.0 tons					
								501.2 tons

targets of opportunity:

		RAF	USAAF
Haamstede	29 April	9.0 tons	
Haamstede	3 May		1.9 tons
North of Alkmaar	2 May		1.9 tons
North West of Edam	2 May		1.9 tons
South of Weesp	2 May		1.9 tons
North of Leerdam	2 May		1.3 tons
Purmerend	3 May		3.8 tons
Baarn	5 May		7.4 tons
		9.0 tons	20.1 tons

total tonnage for all drop zones:

	RAF	USAAF
Waalhaven + Terbregge	3453.6 tons	312.7 tons
Valkenburg airfield	722.5 tons	149.3 tons
Duindigt race course	1333.6 tons	153.1 tons
Ypenburg airfield	1385.9 tons	161.0 tons
Gouda	125.3 tons	–
Schiphol airfield		2184.7 tons
Vogelenzang		349.0 tons
Bergen airfield		161.6 tons
Hilversum		163.1 tons
Utrecht		501.2 tons
targets of opportunity		20.1 tons
	7029.9 tons	4155.8 tons

total in lbs.: 24,058,576 lbs.

Finally free. A crowd of people in Amsterdam.

Appendix F

Ranks in RAF *and* USAAF *compared to similar ranks in the Royal Netherlands Air Force.*

Royal Air Force	US Army Air Force	Nederland
Aircraftman 2nd Class	Private	soldaat
Aircraftman 1st Class	Private 1st Class	soldaat 1ste klasse
Leading Aircraftman	–	–
Corporal	Corporal	korporaal
Sergeant	Sergeant	sergeant
Flight Sergeant	Staff Sergeant	sergeant-majoor
Warrant Officer	Master Sergeant	adjudant-OO
Pilot Officer	2nd. Lieutenant	2de luitenant
Flying Officer	1st. Lieutenant	1 ste luitenant
Flight Lieutenant	Captain	kapitein
Squadron Leader	Major	majoor
Wing Commander	Lieutenant-Colonel	luitenant-kolonel
Group Captain	Colonel	kolonel
Air Commodore	Brigadier-General	commodore
Air Vice-Marshal	Major-General	generaal-majoor
Air Marshal	Lieutenant-General	luitenant-generaal
Air Chief Marshal	General (four star)	generaal
Marshal of the RAF	General (five star)	–
Pilot	Pilot	piloot
Second Pilot	Co-pilot	tweede piloot
Navigator	Navigator	navigator
Flight Engineer	(Flight) Engineer	boordwerktuigkundige
Bomb Aimer	Bombardier	bommenrichter
Observer	–	waarnemer
Front gunner	Nose gunner	neuskoepelschutter
Mid-upper gunner	Top turret gunner	rugkoepelschutter
Rear gunner	Tail turret gunner	staartkoepelschutter
–	Ball turret gunner	buikkoepelschutter
–	Waist gunner	zijluikschutter
Wireless Operator	Radio Operator	radiotelegrafist

Appendix G

The author thanks the people mentioned below for their contribution in the writing of this book by sending documents and photographs, or writing their memories.

Netherlands:
His Royal Highness Prince Bernhard; kolonel A.P. de Jong, KLu.; LtZ1OC W.J.J. Geneste; H. Hofmeester; J. Thoonsen; W. Latenstein van Voorst; Mrs. N. Hanke; Mrs. M. Straathof; H. Engelman; C. Treffers; Mrs. M.M. Plantjé; Mrs. E. van Hall-Davies; A.J. Bus; Mrs. M.B. Wijkhuizen-Labeur; C. Joustra; Mrs. J.M. Corbet-Verheul; J. Vrouwenfelder; J.M. Wentzel; Mrs. P.C. Gerritsen; W.J. van Rijn; J. Dreyer; W. Geutjes; Mrs. L. Karreman-Friederich; Mrs. E.M. op den Kelder-Bos; J.M. Schouten; Jac. W. Kromhout; Mrs. A. v.d. Mik; C.H.J. Helders; drs. A.H. Paape; dr. L. de Jong; E. Somers; J. Zwaan; C. den Haan; Kpt.LtZ. H.J. Grefe; Th.H.P. Lammers; J.G.W. Sluyk; drs. W.A. Fasel; F.W.J. Heukensfeldt-Jansen; C.J.P. Boot; Mrs. Y. Boichel; G.A.M. v.d. Nieuwendijk; sgt.-maj. D. van Leeuwen; sgt.1 K.B. Brandt; lt.-kol. A.M.L. Maas; W. Bot.

No. 1 Group, Bomber Command, Royal Air Force

No. 12 Squadron	: L.W.J. Durrant (GB); F.V. Stanton (CDN); G.J. Cleary (CDN); J. Lowe (GB); E. Stephenson (GB); B. Baillie (NZ); J. Green (NZ); T.J. Rooke (GB); J. Fanish (GB); E. Parker (GB); G. Robinson (GB); A. McInally (USA); A.J. Meade (NZ); J.L. Carruthers (GB); C.W. Hann (CDN); A.S. Matthew (CDN); J.M. Galt (CDN); T. Blythen (GB); R.W. Middlemass (GB); W. Tracey (GB); J.L. Wallace (CDN)
No. 100 Squadron	: R. Moore (GB); D.H. Davies (GB); J. Cook (GB); A.MacCormick (GB); J.H. Rayns (GB); W. Proudpor (GB); D. Robb (CDN); A. Gamble (CDN); C.M. Kerr (CDN); R.G. Ginson (CDN); E. Mosure (CDN); A. White (GB); J.S. Metcalfe (GB)
No. 101 Squadron	: K. Wright (GB); R.F. Upcott (CDN); N.S. Farrow (GB); W.H. Fletcher (GB); N.G. King (GB); W. Packer (GB); F. Bolton (GB); A.P. Philip (NZ); A. Brooker (GB); B. Cooksey (NZ); R. Reid (GB); J. Pickstone (GB); K. Walker (GB); K. Tute (GB); J.E. Bratton (GB)
No. 103 Squadron	: W.E. Monteith (GB); K. Butler (GB); H.P. Cakebread (GB); W. Craigie (GB); R.A. Roberts (GB); E.J. Chad (GB); J. Funnel (GB); R.S. Fettes (GB); S.G. Holtham (GB)
No. 150 Squadron	: G. Bramble (GB); D. Steiner (GB); W.E. Jones (GB); W. Kiley (GB); V. Crook (GB); A. Drinkwater (GB); E.W. Reed (GB); R.L. Spencer (GB); A.R. Ingram (GB); P. Joyce (GB); V. Henderson (AUS); M. Heselton (CDN)
No. 153 Squadron	: C.D. Hill (GB); J. Western (CDN); D. Malone (Bahamas); R. Pease (GB); P.N. Speed (GB); J.H. Harrison (GB); D.S. Broughton (GB); G. Foster (GB); R.S. Murray (GB); J.A. Johns (GB); R.P. Wadsley (GB); K. Percival-Barker (GB); G.L. Coggin (GB); L. Pitt (GB)
No. 166 Squadron	: J. Russell (GB); K. Friswell (GB); A.T. McCullough (CDN); J.R. Hayward (GB); H.G. Ball (GB); J. Huxley-Jones (GB); A. Falconer (SA); D. Bremner (GB); A.R. Twigger (GB)
No. 170 Squadron	: W.H.G. Bunday (GB); W.H. Gibson (GB); J. Whittaker (GB); R. Chandler (GB); D. Underhill (GB); G. Burchell (SA); R. Wooding (GB); B.A. Templeton-Rooke (GB); J. Gould (GB); B. Wallis (GB); J. North (GB); I.F. Cozens (GB); B. Tripp (GB); A. Hargrave (GB); P. Anderson (GB); G.N. Henderson (GB); W. Kiley (GB); G.L. Ward (CDN); J. MacAllister (SA)

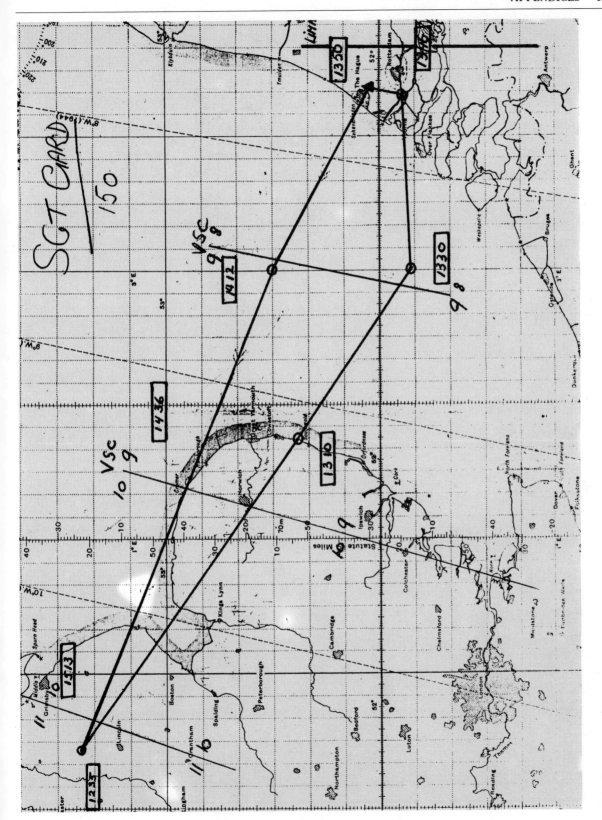

29 April, RAF, Ypenburg.

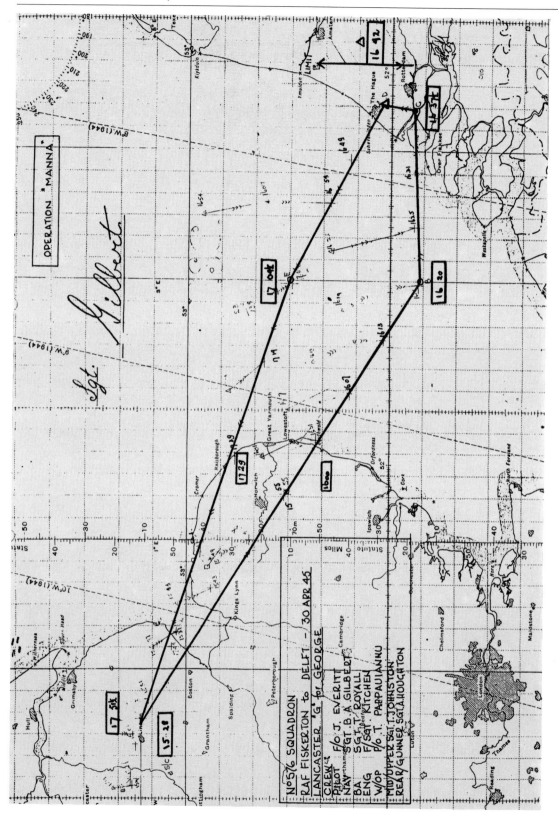

30 April, RAF, Valkenburg.

No. 300 Squadron (Polish)	:	V. Samborski (GB); H. Mindykowski (GB); S. Jeronim (GB); A. Mielnik (AUS); E.A. Oremek (AUS); B. Dyktynski (AUS)
No. 460 Squadron (RAAF)	:	E.D. Leaviss (GB); R.G. Day (AUS); R.J. Turnbull (AUS); R.R. Addison (AUS); S.E. Coverdale (AUS); F.R.W. Milk (AUS); J.P. Hodson (AUS); J.B. Brunt (AUS); H.J. Cameron (AUS); D.T. Williams (AUS); W.F. Dimmick (AUS); J.D. MacCallum (AUS); R.G. Batty (AUS); R.G. Wickham (AUS); A.A. Tapp (AUS); W.J. Mackay (AUS); N.W. Scott (AUS); F.H. Roberts (AUS); T.G. Cahir (AUS); A.J. Durrance (AUS); F.D. Kelly (AUS); A.F. Flanagan (AUS); J.J. McDade (AUS); J.M. Currie (AUS); G. Dorfield (AUS); M.C. Fox (AUS); M.J. Cottage (AUS); N.F. Alexander (AUS); C.J. Smith (AUS); K.R. Archer (AUS); J.N. Stuart (AUS); G.D. Harfield (AUS); A.L. Cohen (AUS); A. Buchanan (AUS); A.E. Jenkins (AUS); H.J. MacNamara (AUS); D.J. Creeper (AUS); F.E. Kowald (AUS); F. Lawrence (AUS); E.H.P. Whitehead (AUS); A.S. Whitmarsh (AUS); P.G. Mason (AUS); R.J. Bruce (AUS); H.G. Johnson (AUS); L.J. Eaton (AUS); R.H. Woodward (AUS); W. Langcake (AUS); A.J. Hodgkinson (AUS); K.W. Bennett (AUS); J.L. Goldworthy (AUS); D.A. James (AUS); J.R. Henderson (AUS); K. Chamberlain (AUS); D.M. Robson (AUS); R.G. Small (AUS); L.F. Bertram (AUS); R.N. Hawkins (AUS); J.G. Wilson (AUS); J.F. Ryan (AUS); W.D. Cullam (AUS); M.A. O'Keeffe (AUS); P.C. Dowling (AUS); D.A. Cook (AUS); T.F. Moustaka (AUS); W.J. Brown (AUS); F.A. d'Alton (AUS); R.B. Hatherley (AUS); C.R. Lyons (AUS); B.W. Kaye (AUS); J.M. Hirst (AUS); L.R. Lewarne (AUS); H.T. Joyce (AUS); L.F. Reid (AUS); N.B. Johnson (AUS); H.T. Kearns (AUS); L.A. Aboud (AUS); J.H. Rock (AUS); D.A. Turner (AUS); D.N. Henderson (AUS); C.T. Crooks (AUS); J.C. Thomson (AUS); L.W.R. Simpson (AUS); P.C. Firkins (AUS); D.K. Teasdale (GB); D.G. Fellowes (GB); L.G. Mottershead (AUS); W. Culsman (AUS); J.M. Currie (AUS); B.T. Marshall (AUS)
No. 550 Squadron	:	J.G.P. Sarll (GB); J. Eveleigh (GB); B. Bell (GB); L.G. Bucknell (GB); E.G. Patterson (GB); G. Placker (GB); F.H. Quick (GB); J. Miles (GB); H.I. Brown (GB); N.J. Horsley (GB); J. Wright (GB); B. Hulse (GB); J. Washington (IRL); E. Barnett (GB); E. Brotherhood (GB); D. Quine (GB); J. Parkinson (GB); B. Wakeford (GB); T. Brown (AUS); T. Moore (GB); N.W. Lewis (GB); E. Redshaw (GB); T. Earney (GB); M.G. Snowball (GB); T. Spicer (GB); R.H. Keevil (GB)
No. 576 Squadron	:	B.A. Gilbert (D); J. Brown (GB); D.A. Thornewell (CDN); D. Bowors (USA); A.W.G. Watson (GB); K.E. Stott (GB); J.W. Everitt (GB); J.C. Hood (AUS); C.F. Lea (AUS); E.A.J. Taylor (GB); B. Lisk (GB); D.R. Herbert (GB); J.E.F. Goodchild (GB); J.R. Pratt (GB)
No. 625 Squadron	:	S.C. Simmonds (GB); J. Bettany (GB); L.W. Liversage (GB); N.G. Nethercott (GB); D.G. McHardy (CDN); W. Birkby (GB); R.E. Stallwood (GB); A.B. Fry (GB); W. Porter (GB)
No. 626 Squadron	:	R.J. Patton (GB); T.J. Rooks (GB); E.J. Hall (GB); G. Robinson (GB); R.J. Griffiths (GB); J. Plenderleith (GB); K.A. Buxton (GB); R.F. Penney (GB); F.A. Bill (GB); F.S. Wardle (GB); J.W. Wyke (AUS)

No. 3 Group, Bomber Command, Royal Air Force

No. 15 Squadron	:	P. Russell (GB); G.H. Hill (GB); R. Davis (GB); D.R. Burgess (GB); R. Heimpel (CDN)
No. 75 Squadron (RNZAF)	:	E.G.W. Gunter (GB); D. Rugg (NZ); B. Dennison (NZ); L. Woodward (NZ); J. Green R.W. Russell (NZ); B.A. Reeve (NZ); A.J. Meade (NZ); T. Matthews (NZ); I. McLellan (NZ); J.S. Carroll (NZ); J. Haworth (NZ); B. Cooksey (NZ); R. MacKenzie (NZ); P. Threvarthen (NZ); W.J. MacMurray (NZ); A.E. Jarvis (NZ); T. Hewitson (NZ); M. Billman (NZ); I.S. Young (NZ); L. McKenna (NZ); D.R. Emms (GB); M. Prince (GB); S.G. Watson (GB); K. Moore (GB); R.R. Craft (GB); T. Murphy (GB); W.R. Brinsden (NZ); L.W. Uden (NZ); W.W. Morgan (NZ); L.A. MacDonald (NZ); G.A. Russell (NZ); L. Woods (NZ); F.N. Snelwod (NZ); V.D. Hendry (NZ); A.P. Philip (NZ); J.A. White (NZ); J. Hunt (GB); L.F. Hurren (GB); R.T. Saul (GB); G.E. Sansom (GB); G. Ford (GB)
No. 90 Squadron	:	J. Davies (GB); T. Saunders (GB); B. Ridgeway (GB); F. Stevenson (GB); R. Gillies (GB); T. Gerrard (GB); K. Proome (Zimbabwe); E. Richardson (GB); K.J. Stidart (GB); R. Jefferey (GB); W.C. McAllister (GB); J.D. Richards (GB); C. Newstead (GB); R.E. Wannop (GB)

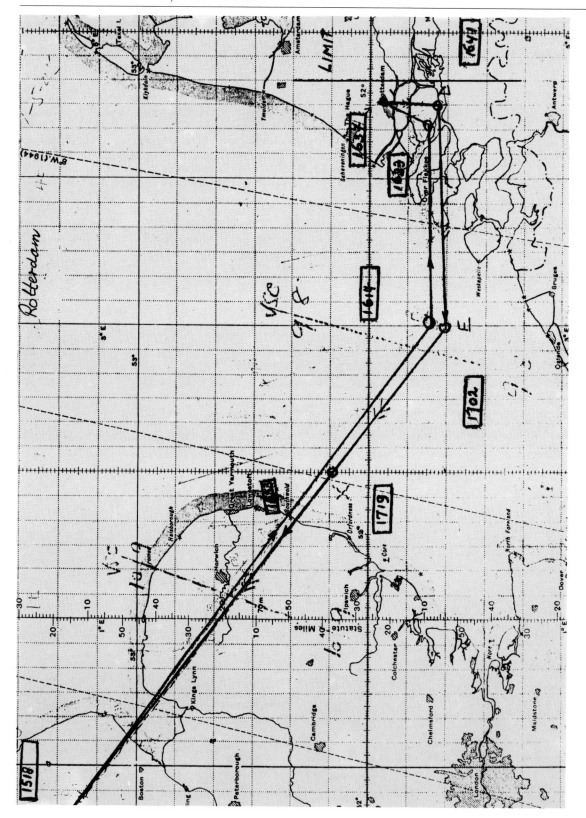

1 May, USAAF, Terbregge.

No. 115 Squadron : P.B. Small (GB); E. Gale (GB); L.V. Rosser (GB); L. Beaman (GB); G.R. Todd (CDN); J. Gildea (GB); J. Walker (GB); F. Fletcher (GB); A. Morrison (GB); J. Towers (GB); B. Leonard (GB); F. Wedge (GB); H.R. Sidney (GB); A.P. Goring (GB); P. Nicholson (GB); J.S. Hewson (GB); W.B. Kane (GB); C.W. Walker (CDN); J.D. Shinning (GB); L.R.G. Armitage (GB); K.W. Simpson (GB); C. McRae (GB); P.J. Atkins (GB); G. Leach (GB); W. Griffith (GB); P.V. Mitchell (GB)

No. 138 Squadron : J.K. Webster (GB); J.W. Harland (GB); B. Russell (GB); K.S. Batchelor (GB)

No. 149 Squadron : F.A. Biggs (GB); K.R. Greenman (GB); J. Fulton (AUS); D. Kebble (GB); F.C. Antell (GB); E. Tomlinson (GB); J.H. Woodward (GB); R.E. Sims (GB); L.J. Kemp (GB); F.E. Horne (GB); E.H.C. Turner (GB); L.G. Comfort (GB); H.G. Bowles (CDN); G. Breen (GB); J.A. White (NZ); K.E. Humphrey (GB); J. Boyle (GB); E. Rosier (GB); D.J. Watkins (GB)

No. 186 Squadron : B.G.W. Haynes (GB); G.R.V. Haynes (GB); R. Kirkin (GB); T.A. Sutton (GB); F.E. Wheat (GB); F.E. Mercer (GB); J.G. Brandon (GB); A. Lewis (GB); F.W. Fennell J.L. Butters (GB)

No. 195 Squadron : K.R. Ketley (GB); D.E.B. Freeman (GB); G. Davies (GB); H.E. Burrows (GB); J.H. Poppleton (GB); E.A. Bristow (GB); H.J.B. Sarsfield-Keily (GB); W. Fairlie (GB); D. Currie (GB); D. Hilton (GB); J. Kerr (GB); L.A. Shaw (GB); H.R. Head (GB); K. Walker (GB); A.F. Page (GB); E.T. Adams (GB); K. Cubitt (GB); D.A. Murfet (GB); G. Calvert (GB); H.M. Sprake (GB); P.G. Richardson (GB); A. Hopkins (AUS); J.L. Jardine (GB); K. Futter (GB); T.C. Kirkwood (GB); W.L. Farquharson (GB)

No. 218 Squadron : P. Irving (GB); R.A. Jell (GB); G. Weaving (GB); J.T. Harding (GB); L.R. Bennett (GB); W. Double (GB); J. Mather (GB); H. Christian (GB); R.A. Horner (GB); P.R.L. Evans (GB); J. Jenkins (GB); R.A. Cowley (AUS); C.A. Eade (GB); P. Dyson (GB); N.H. Bolt (GB); P.J. Legge (GB); J. MacMichael (CDN)

No. 514 Squadron : W. Hough (GB); W.A.E. Peake (GB); G. Mazzina (GB); H.B. Woodcraft (GB); S. Beeves (GB); R.G.K. Price (GB); W.J. Bailey (GB); R. Vipond (GB); G. Sacker (GB); L.A. Adams (NZ); P. Banyard (GB); L.A.J. Holt (GB); J.H. Blandford (GB); F.J. Blandford (GB); R. Slade (GB); R. Kirk (GB); K. Jefferey (GB); W. Hooper (GB); L. King (GB); M.G.T. Allen (GB); C.K. Furdge (GB); T.W. Hurley (CDN); V. Flaterval (CDN)

No. 622 Squadron : B. Harris (GB); A.H. Hallen (GB); K. Wood (GB); C. Malcolm (GB); H.E. Pam (GB); D.C. Carter (GB); M.E.L. Davies (GB); J.P. Swallow (CDN); I.J. Henderson (CDN); R.J. Pople (AUS)

No. 8 Group, Pathfinder Force, Bomber Command, Royal Air Force

No. 7 Squadron : V.G. Smith (GB); R.W. Nairne (GB); W.G. Vincent (GB); D.J. Butters (GB); O.A. Fox (GB); D.J. Rutherford (AUS); K.E. Fettes (GB); E.J. Lisle (AUS); P. Banting (GB); J.A. Lyne (GB); T.W. Reynolds (GB); R. Ormerod (GB); R.H. Nielsen (AUS)

No. 35 Squadron : B.J. Studd (GB); G.J. Etheridge (GB); C. McKinnon (GB); S. Caddle (USA); P. Cooney (USA); P. Saville (GB); D.B. Brown (AUS); A.H. Thomas (GB); K.F. Sheppard (CDN)

No. 105 Squadron : J.C. Sampson (GB); P.W. Plimnett (GB); T. Walmsley (GB); T.P. Lawrensen (GB); C.F. Moller (GB)

No. 109 Squadron : D.N. Smith (GB); E.W.G. Birch (GB); O.J. Pritchard (GB); J.W. Shaw (USA); J. McIntosh (GB)

No. 156 Squadron : L.P. Howell (GB); S. Glasper (GB); S. Menaul (GB); A. Watson (GB); W.I. Davies (CDN); J.R. Hood (GB); T.S. Harris (GB); J.C. Thompson (GB); K.T. Jones (AUS); P.W. Tatham (AUS)

No. 405 Squadron (RCAF) : P.E. Burden (CDN); E. Horner (GB); B. Horsman (GB); J.F. Roberts (CDN); W. Smith (CDN); W.C. McLean (CDN); G.H.K. Begg (CDN); G. Bennett (CDN); H. Campbell (CDN); G. Hastings (CDN); R. Maxwell (CDN); H. Crosby (CDN); F. Gladding (CDN); N. Callerey (CDN); J. Hall (CDN); G. Laslett (CDN); S. Sheritt (CDN); J. Cowell (CDN); R. McGee (CDN); W. Dawe (CDN); D. MacDonald (CDN); H. Czyz (CDN); H. Morton (CDN); T. Jackson (CDN)

No. 582 Squadron : B. Lanning (GB); C.C. Cardwell (GB); J. Walker (GB); G.S. Baker (CDN); K.B. Walker (AUS); E.E. Stocker (GB); J.F. Corrigan (CDN); N. Neilson (CDN); W.T. Evans (AUS)

No. 635 Squadron : J.P.G. Baines (GB); D.W. Beach (GB); B.J.W. Spaul (GB); A. Ashworth (GB)

8th Air Force, 3rd Air Division, United States Army Air Force
13th, 45th, 93rd Combat Wings

95th Bomb Group	: F. Korol; H.J. Dulle; D. Condon; A.N. Braidic; R.J. Belisle; H. Luciano; Z.T. Stanborough; E.B. Scripture; J. Schwarz; W.R. Cook
100th Bomb Group	: F. Quilici; D.S. Eden; R.E. Bragg; R. Powell; W.A. Carleton
390th Bomb Group	: B. Sorensen; R.W. Barnes; F. Denne; H. Giudici; R.H. Calceran; J.A. Moller; J.R. Murray; J.E. Lightfoot jr.; B.J. Holman; R.G. Anker; B. Stvall; W.L. McGrew; L.L. Joos; E.A. Linscheid; R.C. Kownslar; J.F. Krook; J.A. Moller
96th Bomb Group	: R.S. Martin; T.H. Harrison; K. Thaemert; C.M. Cole; A.D. Schaerler; N. Strucken; B.S. Terrey; J.F. Schnieder; H.E. Wiese; S. Hartman; D.C. Kreske; J.L. Higay
388th Bomb Group	: H. Rosenn; R.J. Seney; Ed. Silverman; M.C. Shirley; F.W. Rone; M. Myrick; T.G. Gilkes; C.K. Sharp; V.F. Ficarra; P.H. Bass; P. Rensch; C.S. Rutherford; J.W. DeBruhl; C.R. Seimer; A.T. Brus; J. Schumaker; T.A. Dennis; N.R. Kloter; C.F. Meck; H.J. Ayers; G.A. Palmer; W.C. Ricketts; M. Georgetti; D.C. Biganeiss; L.L. Theimer; H.H. Mallory; M.E. Buckhaults; E. Cohen; R.K. Schneck; R.S. Ward; J. Tryon; J.C. Nagel; N.C. Thompson; R.M. Abrahams; R.J. Zawislack; L. Schweder; T. Crouch; J.A. Fletcher; E. Holtzman; E. Frey; S. Shabman; R. Cooperman; L. Barger; E.B. Petersen; J. Coughlan; H. Wobbema; G.F. Pirnick; A. Serian; D.H. Kalish; J.L. Gross; M. Medicus; L.K. Vale; O. Weislogel; L.H. Kennedy; B. Lund; F.T. Schultz; R. Przybylski; J.R. Anderson; M. Roth; J. Blumenberg; L.L. Smith
45th Bomb Group	: G.P. Remmenga
34th Bomb Group	: H.E. Province; W.E. Creer; E.B. Le Bailly; H.D. Roy; R.L. Summa; C. Cohen; R. Myers
385th Bomb Group	: R.A. Valliere
490th Bomb Group	: J. Milliken
493rd Bomb Group	: W.A. Richards; R.E. Haynes; L. Bird; W. Langley; B. Craig; G. Bliss; G.A. Ford; H.A. Jackson; H.C. Kniffen; G. McCardle; H. Lancaster; J.E. Powers; J. Rude; A. Zimmerman jr.; A.L. Westbrook; K.G. Reinhart jr.
3rd Scouting Force	: D.A. Mullen
Great Britain	: ACM Sir Keith Williamson CAS RAF; Sir Philip Mansfield; Captain A.A. Hensher RN; Gp.Capt. W.S.O. Randle; WC W. Wood; Air Cdre. H.A. Probert; A. Frewin; AM Sir Patrick Hine; W.D. Forney; G.W. Boon; F. Priestley; Air Cdre. A.J.W. Geddes; WC B.F. Hills; J. Walden; Mrs. J. Fish; E. Hine; R. Mack; I.C. MacTaggert; Lt.Col. M. Woodcock RA
United States	: Col. W.C. Haman USAF; Col. F.M. Banks USAF; D.W. Matsenbaugh; O.E. Edgell; C. Worman; Lt.Col. E.M. Solander; C. Butzirius; C. Murray; H.V. Klier; J. Manning
Canada:	: D.H. Gilchrist; R. Stansfield; W.A.B. Douglas; Mrs. B. Wilson; K. Schoenmaker; R. Sanders; E. Grove; L. Lapier; C.H. Graham; C. Ramsay; E. van Heesakker; J.C. McArthur
New-Zealand	: AVM D. Crooks; D.F. Bolt; Mrs. E.J. Benton; Gp.Capt. E.A. Dillon; SL I.J. Dougan; R.T. Bowes; SL R. Springer; Air Cdre. S.C. Quill; G.H. Goss; W.J. Scollay; Sir William Leuchars; WC J.S. Barclay
Australia	: AM F.D. Evans; Dr. J.C.W. Cumes; J.W. Moffat; R. Gilchrist

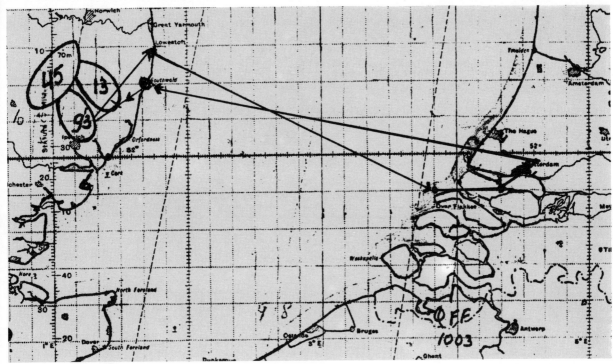

1 May, USAAF, *Terbregge.*

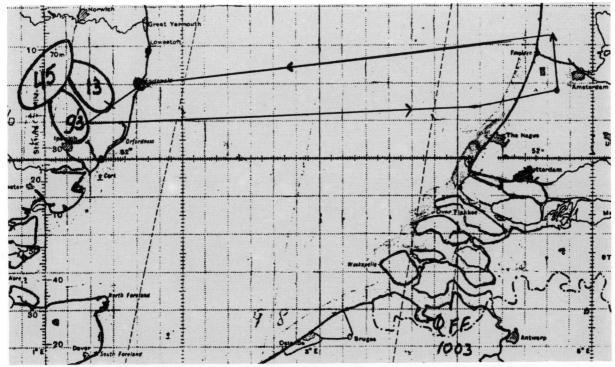

3 May, USAAF, *Schiphol.*

4 May, RAF, Rotterdam.

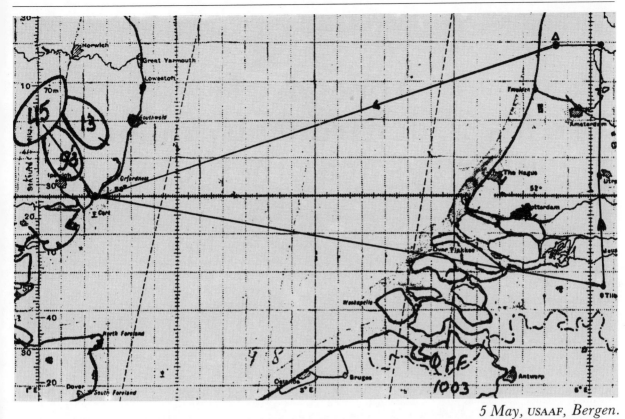

5 May, USAAF, Bergen.

USAAF, *targets of
opportunity:
2 May –
1 south of Alk-
maar;
2 northwest of
Edam;
3 south of Weesp;
4 south of Leerdam;
3 May –
5 north of Purme-
rend;
6 Haamstede Air-
field;
7 near Amersfoort;
8 Dordrecht.
On 29 April a
Lancaster flying
on three engines
dropped bags near
Haamstede.*

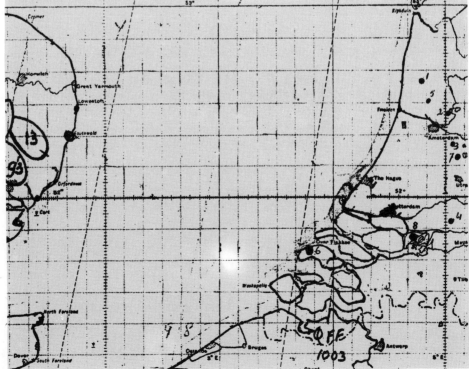

Appendix H
Archives, departments, municipal authorities and other institutes

Netherlands:
Municipal authorities and archives of Rotterdam; The Hague; Wassenaar; Leiden; Gouda; Hilversum; Utrecht; Alkmaar; Purmerend; Westerschouwen; Leerdam; Weesp; Amsterdam; Katwijk; Bergen; Archives of South Holland; the burgomaster of Goedereede; Netherlands Institute for War Documentation; National War and Resistance Museum Overloon; Department of Air Force History; North Sea Ferries; Ambassies of Great Britain; the United States of America, New Zealand; Australia; Canada; Provincial Military Command South Holland; Committee for the Allied Cemetery Bergen; Topographic Service of the Department of Defence; Air War Bulletin Group; Foundation for the National Commemoration of the Liberation

United Kingdom:
Air Historical Branch MoD; Public Record Office; Imperial War Museum; Royal Air Force Museum; BBC Written Archives Centre; BBC Radio Humberside; The Polish Air Force Association; The Royal Air Forces Association; No. 170 Squadron Reunion Association; RAF Film Production Unit; Her Majesty's Embassy in London; RAF Personnel Management Centre; RAF Scampton; Air Crew Association; Air Gunners Association; No. 7 Squadron Association; The Milderhall Register; The Wickenby Register; The Pathfinder Association; The Bomber Command Association; The Little Staughton Pathfinder Association

United States of America:
Air Force Museum; Albert F. Simpson Historical Research Center; Air Force Magazine; DAVA; Military Personnel Records Center; National Air and Space Museum Smithsonian Institute; Boeing Inc.; National Archives and Records Service; Office of the Air Force History; 1361st Audio-Visual Squadron; Aerospace Historian; USAF Military Personnel Center; The Eight Air Force Historical Society; 7th Photo Group Association; 95th Bomb Group Association; 100th Bomb Group Association; Air Force Office of Public Affairs; Air Force Times; 490th Bomb Group Association

German Federal Republic:
Volksbund Deutsche Kriegsgräberfürsorge e.V. (German Federal Wargraves Commission); Bundesarchiv; Militärarchiv

Canada:
Canadian Warplane Heritage Inc.; Canadian Corps Association; Army, Navy and Air Force Veterans; Public Archives of Canada; Royal Canadian Military Institute; National Defence Headquarters; Legion Magazine; Bomber Command Association (Canada); Royal Canadian Air Forces Association; Royal Canadian Legion

New-Zealand:
Ministry of Defence; Office of the Chief of the Air Staff; No. 75 (NZ) Squadron Association; Royal New Zealand Air Force Association; Brevet Club of New Zealand; N.Z.; Returned Servicemens Association

Australia:
Department of Defence; The Office of the Chief of the Air Staff; Royal Air Forces Association; Returned Services League of Australia; No. 460 Squadron Association; Polish Air Force Association-Victoria Branch

Appendix I
Bibliography

W.H. Baarle	*De Slag om B2* (Den Haag, 1945)
Max Blokzijl	*Ik zei tot ons volk* (Utrecht, 1943)
M. Brave-Maks	*Prins Bernhard in oorlogstijd* (Amsterdam, 1962)
W.S. Churchill	*De Tweede Wereldoorlog,* dln. 9 en 10 (Amsterdam, 1979)
J. Drummond	*Malnutrition and Starvation in Western Netherlands,* 2 vol. (Den Haag, 1948)
D.D. Eisenhower	*Kruistocht door Europa* (Den Haag, 1952)
K. Groen	*Er heerst orde en rust . . .* (Nijmegen, 1979)
Alden Hatch	*Prins Bernhard* (Amsterdam, 1962)
H.M. Hirschfeld	*Herinneringen uit de bezettingstijd* (Amsterdam, 1960)
L. de Jong	*De Bezetting,* dl. 5 (Amsterdam, 1965)
L. de Jong	*Het Koninkrijk der Nederlanden in de Tweede Wereldoorlog,* dl. 10b, 2e helft (Den Haag, 1982)
J.G. Onderwater	*En toen was het stil . . .* (Baarn, 1981)
H. v.d. Zee	*De Hongerwinter* (Amsterdam, 1979)
N. Scheepmaker	*Het Zweedse Wittebrood* (Baarn, z.d.)
	Dagboekfragmenten (Amsterdam, 1954)
M.J.F. Bowyer	*Action Stations,* dl. 1 (Cambridge, 1979)
H.St.G. Saunders	*Royal Air Force 1939-1945,* III (London, 1954)
Percy Ernst Schramm	*Kriegstagebuch des Oberkommandos der Wehrmacht,* Band IV (München, 1982)
Col. C.P. Stacey	*The Victory Campaign,* III (Ottawa, 1960)
H.P. Willmott	B-*17 Flying Fortress* (London, 1980)
R.A. Freeman	B-*17 Fortress at War* (Shepperton, 1977)
R.A. Freeman	*Airfields of the Eighth; then en now* (London, 1978)
R.A. Freeman	*The Mighty Eightht War Diary* (London, 1981)
R.A. Freeman	*The Mighty Eighth* (London, 1978)
P.J.R. Moyes	*Bomber Squadrons of the* RAF *and their aircraft* (London, 1964)
M. Garbett & B. Goulding	*The Lancaster at War,* (London, 1978)
M. Garbett & B. Goulding	*Lancaster at War,* 2 (London, 1979)
C. Bowyer	*Path Finders at War* (London, 1977)
B. Robertson	*Lancaster – The Story of a Famous Bomber* (Watford, 1977)
Sir C. Webster & N. Frankland	*The Strategic Air Offensive against Germany 1939-1945,* VOL. III (London, 1961)
L.F. Ellis	*Victory in the West,* II (London, 1962)
P.A. Veldheer	*Daar komen de Canadezen* (Arnhem, 1982)
D. Marley	*The Daily Telegraph Story of the war,* dln. 4 en 5 (London, 1946)
H. van Gelder	*Mei 1945* (Bussum, 1980)
H.J. Neuman	*Arthur Seyss-Inquart* (Utrecht, 1967)
Sir Francis de Guingand	*Operation Victory* (London, 1947)
Zena Stein a.o.	*Famine and Human Development; the Dutch hungerwinter of 1944-1945* (London, 1975)

Appendix J
Picture Credits

The publisher tried to reach all copyrightholders, in most cases successfully. However we ask you to contact the publisher, if illustrations have been used without prior consent of the copyrightholder.